First Line of Defense

Ambassadors, Embassies and American Interests Abroad

Edited by Robert V. Keeley

The American Academy of Diplomacy
Washington. D.C.

The American Academy of Diplomacy
1800 K. Street, N.W., Suite 1014
Washington, DC 20006

This project was funded by a grant to the Academy from the Nelson B. Delavan Foundation

ISBN 0-9679108-0-3
Library of Congress Control Number: 131694
Published in the United States of America

Dedication

This book is dedicated to the men and women who in the past and still today have had the task of carrying out the myriad functions of diplomacy that serve to protect the vital interests of the American nation and people in our relations with the rest of the world. Many were and are members of the Foreign Service of the United States who spend their careers in diplomacy. Others are in many departments and agencies of our federal government who serve abroad in our diplomatic and consular missions for parts of their careers. Still others are private American citizens who serve for a time as presidential appointees to diplomatic positions in the service of their country. Finally there are the loyal citizens of other countries who help staff our missions abroad with uncommon devotion. These public servants of the nation are thought to live glamorous lives, but the truth is that they often live in conditions of great hardship and even danger. They all devote their lives to serving the nation, many of them at times risk their lives, and far too many in recent years have lost their lives in that service. This book does not emphasize those sacrifices, but it tries to tell the story of what these men and women actually do in their service around the world, and of the pride they take in their work on behalf of their compatriots.

Contents

Acknowledgments

The American Academy of Diplomacy is grateful to the following persons who assisted in this project. The senior diplomatic and other governmental positions they held are listed after their names.

- Michael Armacost—Ambassador to Philippines and Japan; Under Secretary of State for Political Affairs.
- James K. Bishop—Ambassador to Niger, Liberia, and Somalia.
- James J. Blanchard—Ambassador to Canada; Governor of Michigan.
- Robert R. Bowie—Assistant Secretary of State for Policy Planning; Counselor of the State Department.
- Frank C. Carlucci—Ambassador to Portugal; Deputy Secretary and Secretary of Defense; National Security Adviser; Deputy Director of the Central Intelligence Agency; Deputy Secretary of Health, Education, and Welfare; Deputy Director of the Office of Management and Budget; Director of the Office of Economic Opportunity.
- Elinor G. Constable—Ambassador to Kenya; Assistant Secretary of State for Oceans and International Environmental and Scientific Affairs.
- Robert S. Dillon—Ambassador to Lebanon; Deputy Commissioner General of UNRWA.
- Richard N. Gardner—Ambassador to Italy and Spain.
- William C. Harrop—Ambassador to Guinea, Kenya, Seychelles, Zaire, and Israel; Inspector General of the State Department and the Foreign Service.
- Arthur W. Hummel Jr.—Ambassador to Burma, Ethiopia, Pakistan, and China; Assistant Secretary of State for East Asian and Pacific Affairs.
- L. Craig Johnstone—Ambassador to Algeria; Director of the State Department's Office of Resources, Plans, and Policy.
- James R. Jones—Ambassador to Mexico; Member of the U.S. Congress.
- Robert V. Keeley—Charge d'Affaires in Uganda; Ambassador to Mauritius, Zimbabwe, and Greece.
- L. Bruce Laingen—Ambassador to Malta; Charge d'Affaires in Iran.
- Stephen Low—Ambassador to Zambia and Nigeria; Director of the Foreign Service Institute.
- Walter Mondale—Ambassador to Japan; Vice President of the United States; U.S. Senator.
- Langhorne A. Motley—Ambassador to Brazil; Assistant Secretary of State for Inter-American Affairs.

- John Negroponte—Ambassador to Honduras, Mexico, and Philippines; Deputy National Security Adviser; Assistant Secretary of State for Oceans and International Environmental and Scientific Affairs.
- Robert B. Oakley—Ambassador to Zaire, Somalia, and Pakistan; Director of the State Department's Office for Combatting Terrorism.
- Edward J. Perkins—Ambassador to Liberia, South Africa, the United Nations, and Australia; Director General of the Foreign Service.
- Thomas R. Pickering—Ambassador to Jordan, Nigeria, El Salvador, Israel, the United Nations, India, and the Russian Federation; Executive Secretary of the State Department; Assistant Secretary of State for Oceans and International Environmental and Scientific Affairs; Under Secretary of State for Political Affairs.
- Nicholas Platt—Ambassador to Zambia and Philippines; Executive Secretary of the State Department.
- Anthony C. E. Quainton—Ambassador to the Central African Republic, Nicaragua, Kuwait, and Peru; Director of the State Department's Office for Combatting Terrorism; Assistant Secretary of State for Diplomatic Security; Director General of the Foreign Service.
- Edward M. Rowell—Ambassador to Bolivia, Portugal, and Luxembourg.
- Mary A. Ryan—Ambassador to Swaziland; Assistant Secretary of State for Consular Affairs.
- Raymond G. H. Seitz—Ambassador to the United Kingdom; Assistant Secretary of State for European Affairs; Executive Assistant to the Secretary of State.
- Harry W. Shlaudeman—Ambassador to Venezuela, Peru, Argentina, Brazil, and Nicaragua; Assistant Secretary of State for Inter-American Affairs; Ambassador at Large.
- Robert S. Strauss—Ambassador to the Soviet Union; Special Trade Representative; Special Representative of the President for Middle East Peace Negotiations.
- Frank Wisner—Ambassador to Zambia, Egypt, Philippines, and India; Under Secretary of State; Deputy Under Secretary of Defense.
- John S. Wolf—Ambassador to Malaysia.
- Warren Zimmermann—Ambassador to Yugoslavia; Ambassador and Head of Delegation to the Conference on Security and Cooperation in Europe; Director of the State Department's Bureau of Refugee Programs.

The editor acknowledges with thanks the valuable editorial assistance of Margery Boichel Thompson and Michal M. Keeley, who made this book much more readable. The Academy also notes with thanks the important role in bringing this project to fruition of Maria St. Catherine Sharpe, Assistant to the President of the Academy, Matthew Farber and Dan Houston, interns from George Washington University, and volunteer Andreas Zierold.

Duties of the Ambassador and of His Staff

The obligations and responsibilities of an ambassador are laid out with clarity and precision in U.S. law (22USC3927):

"Chief of Mission

(a) Duties

Under the direction of the President, the chief of mission to a foreign country

(1) shall have full responsibility for the direction, coordination, and supervision of all Government executive branch employees in that country (except for employees under the command of a United States military commander); and

(2) shall keep fully and currently informed with respect to all activities and operations of the Government within that country and shall insure that all government branch employees in that country (except for employees under the command of a United States military commander) comply fully with all the applicable directives of the chief of mission.

(b) Duties of agencies with employees in foreign countries

Any executive branch agency having employees in a foreign country shall keep the chief of mission to that country fully and currently informed with respect to all activities and operations of its employees in that country, and shall insure that all of its employees in that country (except for employees under the command of a United States military commander) comply fully with all applicable directives of the chief of mission."

Preface

The purpose of this publication is quite straightforward. It is to try to answer the question of whether and why we still need ambassadors and embassies to carry out our foreign relations at overseas posts, given the many changes in communications and long-distance travel that have occurred as we begin the third millennium, as well as the new diplomatic environment growing out of the end of the Cold War. What is more, as embassies have increasingly become the targets of terrorist violence as vulnerable symbols of countries and governments that certain groups wish to attack, many have begun to question their value or even their necessity.

This book is a project of the American Academy of Diplomacy, a 100-member organization of retired career and noncareer diplomats who served as ambassadors in important overseas missions, and of other senior officials involved with foreign affairs such as former secretaries of state and senior diplomatic, congressional, military, and intelligence officials who served in leadership positions in recent administrations.

The book resulted from the collaborative effort of about 30 former American ambassadors, most of them retired. They provided their insights on the questions examined herein and their personal recollections as heads of diplomatic missions, many in written form, some in interviews, and a number as participants in an all-day symposium hosted by the Brookings Institution on February 8, 1999. These "co-authors" and other participants are identified by name in the chapters that follow, with pertinent biographical information provided in accompanying footnotes, as well as under "Acknowledgments" on pages vi and vii.

The introductory chapter looks at challenges to the overall role, obligations, and responsibilities of a U.S. ambassador and his or her embassy.* The following chapters offer evidence that ambassadors have not become obsolete and examine the important roles that ambassadors and their embassies currently play in (a) exercising leadership not only

---

* Throughout the rest of this book we will dispense with the "he or she" and "his or her" formulations; use of the masculine pronoun alone does not mean that all ambassadors are male. Since the 1930s scores of women, career and noncareer, have served as ambassadors.

over the personnel, policies, and programs of all U.S. agencies represented in the embassy but also over the private American community living and working in the host country, especially in the realm of protecting the welfare of American citizens and interests; (b) influencing foreign policies determined in Washington by providing well-informed analyses of the host country environment, as well as influencing the positions of the host government through direct communication and public diplomacy; (c) managing crisis situations resulting from natural disasters, civil wars, terrorist attacks, and other such life-threatening situations; and (d) supporting and promoting American business interests abroad, in investment, trade, and contracting, to ensure fairness in treatment, transparency, and access. Underlying all else is the urgent need to have adequate resources to support effective U.S. diplomacy. A final chapter summarizes the conclusions of this study.

Much of what follows will appear self-evident to the professional diplomat. However, this book is aimed at a wider audience, not only of policy makers at all levels of government but also of their constituents, who may not be as aware of the role played by U.S. diplomacy. It is apparent that in recent years Americans have increasingly turned inward, focusing almost exclusively on domestic concerns to the neglect of an interest in foreign affairs that was prominent, if not pre-eminent, during the 40-plus years of the Cold War. It is to that wider audience that this book makes the case that ambassadors and embassies are today as important as they ever were, perhaps more so now that we are beginning to appreciate the difficulty of protecting America's welfare and interests in the ever more complex and volatile post-Cold War world.*

---

* Three other studies recently published in Washington have addressed the subject of refo.ming American diplomacy for the new century. They are:

1. *Reinventing Diplomacy in the Information Age*, Center for Strategic and International Studies, October 1998.

2. *Equipped for the Future--Managing U.S. Foreign Affairs in the 21st Century*, Henry L. Stimson Center, October 1998.

3. *America's Overseas Presence in the 21st Century*, The Report of the Overseas Presence Advisory Panel, U.S. Department of State, November 1999.

Ambassadorial Roles
Then And Now

Robert Strauss was not a diplomat when he was appointed ambassador to the Soviet Union by President Bush. His selection was a surprise—to Strauss himself as much as to the American public—for he was a Democrat, a leader of the opposition party. His expertise and skills were in law and business, politics and government. He knew very well how Washington worked, but not so much about the Soviet Union, the movers and shakers in Moscow, Russian history and culture, Communism, or Cold War strategy and tactics.*

When he arrived in Moscow, as he tells the story, he had been sent hurriedly to his post because of a crisis there. In the midst of the attempted coup against President Mikhail Gorbachev in August 1991, it was unclear whether it would succeed and what it would mean for relations with the United States. Tanks filled the streets, and Gorbachev was in captivity in Crimea. Strauss's basic instruction from his superiors in Washington was to develop as close a personal relationship as possible with the Russian leader, and for that purpose his experiences in American politics dealing with contending personalities and factions, and competing candidates, gave him just the interpersonal skills he needed. In Washington Strauss had been given some prepared remarks from President Bush to the Russian people that the State Department hoped he would find an occasion to use.

But on arrival, caught in an uncertain and turbulent situation, his first instinct was to seek the advice of former Soviet Ambassador to Washington Anatoly Dobrynin, his friend of many years in Washington. He got through on the telephone to Dobrynin, who said that from what he had been hearing the whole thing might blow over in the next 24 hours. They agreed that Strauss's wisest course as the new ambassador would be to "keep his mouth shut and do nothing." So Strauss phoned Secretary of State James Baker and Deputy Secretary of State Lawrence Eagleburger and suggested, without revealing whose advice he had

---

* Ambassador Strauss was not, however, lacking in diplomatic experience. He had previously served presidents as special trade representative and as special representative for Middle East peace negotiations.

sought, that our best policy was to do nothing and wait the situation out. The coup was over a day later, President Gorbachev had returned to Moscow, and Boris Yeltsin had emerged as a proven leader and a democratic force. Strauss earned high marks in Washington for his first bit of advice from Moscow and his handling of that crisis.

A few days later a memorial service was held in Moscow for three young men who had died defending the pro-democracy forces in front of the Russian White House. The ambassadors of various countries were to gather in a reserved area of the public square in a show of unity and support for President Gorbachev. As he approached the area, Strauss observed a flatbed truck with a microphone mounted on a pole parked in a section of the square opposite from the area where the ambassadors were gathering.

Sensing an opportunity to use the prepared remarks from President Bush to the Russian people that he had been given in Washington, Strauss left his ambassadorial colleagues, crossed some security ropes despite the objections of security personnel assigned to protect him, and approached the flatbed truck. Behind it was gathered the entire Russian establishment, from the head of the KGB to Andrei Sakharov's wife, Elena Bonner; the mayor of Moscow, Gavril Popov; and President Gorbachev. Strauss had met Gorbachev several times previously, at dinners and other functions in Washington, but of course not yet in Moscow. He reintroduced himself, was greeted warmly, and received an apology from Gorbachev that he had not been able to welcome him to Russia sooner—"because I have been busy," said Gorbachev, smiling. He said he would arrange for Strauss to present his credentials in a few days and that, in the meantime, he should act as if that had already been done.

Strauss thanked the president and asked who would be speaking that day. Gorbachev said it would be a short service, with a Russian Orthodox priest, a rabbi, and another Christian minister—representing the faiths of the three young men who had died. Popov and Gorbachev also would each speak for a few minutes. Thinking quickly, Strauss said he would like to be added to the program so that he could deliver a message from President Bush. Gorbachev looked uncertain, so the ambassador immediately added: "I can't think of anything more important for you and your country than to have the U.S. ambassador standing before 300,000 people in this square and expressing the support of the American president and the American government for Mikhail Gorbachev." Gorbachev looked up sharply and said, "Mr. Ambassador, you will speak just before me."

Strauss's political instincts had served him well. He turned to Vera Murray, his longtime assistant whom he had brought with him to Moscow, and said: "Vera, this reminds me of a Democratic Party convention. Everybody is in charge and nobody's in charge. That's why I pushed myself onto the program." President Bush's statement was read before 300,000 people in the square and was carried throughout the Soviet Union and around the world to an anxious audience still uncertain about the situation in Moscow. Had there not been an American ambassador on the spot that day, even one who had yet to present his credentials, this opportunity would have been missed entirely.

How Technology Has Affected Diplomacy

For much of the 19th century our diplomatic envoys serving abroad as the president's personal representatives to various kings, queens, presidents, and other potentates communicated with their headquarters at home—the Department of State and the White House—by letters or despatches carried by ships traversing the oceans. These envoys received their instructions on America's foreign policies and how to deal with foreign governments by the same means. It is legendary that some of these envoys were rarely heard from, and a very few may never have been heard from, acting strictly on their own understanding of what they should be doing. Later on, with the advent of the radio telegraph and the transoceanic telephone cable, the speed of communications vastly accelerated. Instead of the weeks once required for an exchange of communications, headquarters and embassies could be in daily or even hourly touch with each other, limited only by cost and the need to encrypt sensitive messages.

Communications technology today has taken another quantum leap with the availability of worldwide satellites, cell phones, computers, secure telephones, and the Internet and its e-mail capability. These new devices have speeded up our communications capabilities, but they have also brought about a downside in that they have made it more difficult for our chiefs of mission to exercise their responsibility to coordinate the policies laid down by Washington and implemented abroad under their direction.

These technological changes have also raised the understandable question of whether and why our president needs a personal representative, for example, living in London, accredited to the Court of St. James's, in order to communicate effectively with our close ally, the government of the United Kingdom. He can simply pick up the phone and talk personally with his close friend, the prime minister of Great Britain. In fact he does that frequently, and there is no language barrier, except the normal one between two people who speak different dialects of English.

Such communications are not limited to close allies. Our president and our secretary of state are known to confer frequently by telephone with other allied leaders, as well as chiefs of state and government of countries with which we are not allied, and even of countries with which we are having problems getting along, and sometimes with leaders of countries with which we are having major disputes. Suppose they don't have a secure phone handy and are concerned that someone might be listening in. They can always turn to their computers and send a personal e-mail message. It is not beyond conception that a group of these world leaders might organize an Internet "chat room" where they could palaver to their hearts' content, a "Group of Seven" chat room, or a NATO chat room.

Another revolution in communications that has affected diplomacy is satellite television, especially an all-news channel like CNN that reports all day long on events happening all over the world, with an immediacy and impact that have profoundly influenced information transfer and decision making everywhere, including Washington. It used to be that senior and more junior diplomats working in Washington at the State Department handling relations with various countries and regions started their workday checking the *New York Times* and the *Washington Post* and perhaps other newspapers to see what was being reported in the media about the countries and regions they were responsible for following. In some cases that is how they got their news first, sometimes before the embassies they were in communication with had reported on the same developments.

Policy makers, press spokesmen, and others interacting with the media, the Congress, and the public had to react, as best they could, to whatever events were being publicly reported about the countries they were "responsible" for. Now they hear first what is reported on CNN or other news channels and have to react to that. The fact that a situation is reported on CNN makes it a focus of diplomatic attention. The technological shift from newspapers to electronic media has had a major impact because the latter is nearly simultaneous with the news being reported, and is made up of visual images that are emotionally gripping. (Just compare the news coverage of World War II before the advent of television with the coverage of the Vietnam War.)

There is nothing particularly benign about this shift to electronic media. Events reported on CNN receive an emphasis that may be way beyond their actual significance, whereas things that go unreported are relegated to a secondary or tertiary status and may be seriously neglected, even though they may be at least as serious and consequential. The result is that the diplomatic agenda is now often driven by the images on television, which can at times oversimplify, magnify, or exaggerate events in ways that distort reality as much as report it.

The changes affecting diplomacy in the area of transportation have been just as dramatic. With the advent of jet aircraft, it became possible for world leaders to fly all over the globe to meet with colleagues singly or in groups. Summit conferences of varying sets of world leaders have now become common, and our president and secretary of state regularly attend meetings of leaders of Latin American nations, Asia-Pacific countries, and NATO members and associates, as well as conferences on economic problems, nuclear proliferation, population control, women's rights, trade issues, and a host of other international concerns. Globe-trotting is a major part of the jobs of both the president and the secretary of state, and has been so since the administration of Dwight Eisenhower and John Foster Dulles. In 1997 Secretary of State Madeleine Albright's trips abroad included visits to 52 countries. In 1998 she visited 35 countries, and in 1999 the figure was 39. These must be new records for foreign travel by a secretary of state. An interesting corollary to the ability of senior officials to jet around the world promoting their policies through personal contacts with their counterparts abroad is that jet aircraft also enable our ambassadors to return to Washington fairly frequently to lobby their bosses on policy issues affecting the countries where they are serving (see accounts by Frank Carlucci and Frank Wisner in chapter 3).

Another phenomenon of modern diplomacy facilitated by jet aircraft—probably initiated by Cyrus Vance in the Lyndon Johnson administration and later popularized by Henry Kissinger—came to be known as "shuttle diplomacy," with the senior American diplomat flying from capital to capital of the principal nations involved to try to settle or at least defuse some conflict. A parallel technique that has become routine is for the president or secretary of state to appoint a special envoy to deal personally with a problematic region, for example, Dennis Ross with the Middle East "peace process," Richard Holbrooke with the turmoil in the breakup of Yugoslavia, George Mitchell with Northern Ireland, and Robert Gallucci with North Korea.

Do all of these changes diminish the importance or relevance of ambassadors assigned to individual countries? It is true that the personal involvement of high-level officials or special envoys to some extent over-rides the role traditionally played by ambassadors as the interlocutors who have provided a human channel of direct communications between and among governments. But it can also be argued that because the shrinking of the globe has made relationships among nations more complex, with greater potential dangers to world order and security, ambassadors have more work to do than ever before, making their presence on the ground in foreign capitals essential.

American Diplomacy Shortchanged

William Harrop, a career Foreign Service officer and five-time ambassador,* articulates the position of those who deplore the severe reductions in the funding of our foreign relations. Harrop notes that everyone seems to agree that the United States is now the only global power. Other nations look to us for leadership and tend to procrastinate until the United States has taken a stand. Yugoslavia is a salient example. Kosovo is on Europe's doorstep, not ours, but our European allies waited for us to decide that NATO must take military action. Then we persuaded them to join us. Leadership is exercised through diplomacy, and effective diplomacy requires adequate funding.

The State Department and Foreign Service have greater burdens than ever before—more governments to deal with, more information to analyze, expanded telecommunications, and increased public involvement. The international agenda for the 21st century is more complex than it was during the Cold War. Then we measured the world in a bipolar context and deployed our superior economic resources and military technology primarily to contain the Soviets.

The new problems, Ambassador Harrop argues, such as the proliferation of weapons of mass destruction, complex trading rules and intellectual property rights, terrorism, traffic in drugs, world environmental pollution, regional ethnic and religious conflicts, refugee displacements, human rights violations, and an increasingly global economy, cannot be resolved unilaterally by even a global power. Such questions require communication with other peoples, building coalitions of concerned governments to work together to address issues that ignore national borders. In short, they demand diplomacy.

Not long ago the United States and its NATO allies were at war in

---

* To Guinea, Kenya, Seychelles, Zaire, and Israel. He also served in Washington as inspector general of the State Department and the Foreign Service.

Kosovo, Harrop points out, and other complicated challenges continue to impend around the globe. But the president has requested inadequate appropriations for conducting American foreign policy in recent fiscal years, barely half of what was allocated in 1985. And Congress has consistently appropriated less than the president's already deficient requests. Further cuts are projected for the coming five years.

The State Department has been closing American embassies and consulates abroad, in part because appropriations are insufficient to make them secure or to maintain them adequately. Yet America needs representatives in overseas capitals. We cannot foresee when we might have to seek the cooperation of another country (even a small one), when we might require use of a particular foreign airfield to interdict drug shipments or to deploy U.S. forces, when securing a nation's favorable vote in the United Nations might prove crucial, where a major new mineral deposit might be discovered, when an American businessman or tourist might need urgent help. U.S. representation can be inexpensive and modest—consisting of just two or three diplomats—but appropriations are necessary.

Harrop emphasizes that the lack of adequate funding has even extended to neglect of providing a high level of security for our diplomatic personnel and premises abroad. The accountability review boards chaired by Admiral William Crowe that analyzed the terrorist bombings of the American embassies in Nairobi, Kenya, and Dar es Salaam, Tanzania, concluded that the disasters were the result of failure over the past 10 years to provide the resources needed to protect the people who serve the United States abroad. The boards forcefully recommended appropriations of $1.4 billion annually for a decade to construct safer embassies, train personnel, and procure modern equipment. The boards rightly emphasized that these resources must be additional to regular State Department appropriations, since there would be no conceivable way to shift to security use funds that were already inadequate for diplomatic operations.

National security is supported and defended by our diplomatic experts, our intelligence professionals, and our armed forces. Their interlocking functions constitute a system analogous to the meshing of land, sea, and air components within the military. Diplomacy serves as prevention, our first line of defense. If we can settle international differences through discussion and negotiation, we do not have to risk the lives of our servicemen and women. But how many people know that since Vietnam more ambassadors than generals have been killed in the line of duty?

After an urgent appeal by the Joint Chiefs of Staff in late 1998, the administration and Congress began to reverse the sharp reductions made in the national defense budget since 1991, when the Cold War ended. Appropriations for intelligence have also now been augmented. Ambassador Harrop concludes that the national interest urgently calls for a similar reversal of the relatively much deeper cuts in the funding of American diplomacy, which is just as much a component of our national security as are our military forces and intelligence operations.

The Statutory Role of the Ambassador

Tony Motley draws on his experience as a senior U.S. diplomat and Foreign Service Institute (FSI) instructor to spell out the mission and duties of an ambassador.* The role of the ambassador in the formulation and conduct of foreign policy, he explains, is shaped by several things: his obligations under law and presidential directive; the changing nature of the objectives and focus of foreign policy; the interest—or lack thereof—displayed by the various segments of the U.S. body politic, including the White House, Congress, the media, think tanks, and the public; and finally, how the individual ambassador views his role and sets out to fulfill it.

Technological changes in the means and rapidity of communications and transportation have relegated ambassadors to the role of secondary messenger in some people's minds. Nothing could be further from the truth. It is precisely the loss of the luxury of time for contemplation, combined with the overload of information—but not necessarily knowledge or understanding—that has enhanced the role of the ambassador. It is the ambassador, as the president's full-time personal representative on the ground, who most likely will have not only the latest information but also the background and context to best describe the situation, propose the recommended actions to meet U.S. objectives, and then carry out the decision that ensues. The ambassador is in the best position to quickly synthesize all the complicated, and sometimes competing, factors and interests into a coherent course of action.

The obligations and responsibilities of an ambassador are laid out with remarkable clarity and precision in U.S. law (see quotation on page viii). The legal foundation is sweeping, specific, and daunting. Unlike the man-

---

* He was ambassador to Brazil and assistant secretary of state for inter-American affairs and since 1985 has co-chaired the FSI's ambassadorial seminar, a mandatory course for all first-time ambassadors.

dates of cabinet secretaries, it covers all agencies. That is not to say that ambassadors have more responsibilities than cabinet officers, but their mandate clearly crosses bureaucratic lines and covers all executive branch personnel. To ensure that this mandate is understood by all agencies in Washington and the field, the law in section (b) places their employees serving abroad under the command of the American ambassador.

This codified responsibility, and the attendant authorities granted, are reinforced by a letter from the president to each new ambassador, with a companion memo instructing all agency heads in Washington to comply, that further delineates specific areas of interest to the current president. There is a rich history of these letters, going back to President Kennedy, who created the "country team" concept with the ambassador in charge,* and each letter builds on the previous ones to clarify any misinterpretation of the law by agencies or individuals serving at that time. For example, extracts from the latest letter from President Clinton leave no doubts that he puts all executive branch employees residing abroad under the direction and supervision of an ambassador:

"This encompasses all American and foreign-national personnel, in all employment categories, whether direct-hire or contract, full- or part-time, permanent or temporary.

"You have the right to see all communications to or from mission elements, however transmitted, except those specifically exempted by law or executive decision."

Another portion of Clinton's letter draws on President Bush's earlier letter and clearly delineates who can give instructions or "orders" to ambassadors:

"The only authorized channel for instructions to you is from him [the secretary of state] or me. There are only two exceptions: (1) If I personally instruct you to use a privacy channel; or (2) If the Secretary instructs you to use a non-State channel."

In summary, the law clearly sets out responsibilities to direct, coordinate, and supervise executive branch employees and their activities overseas in a manner unthinkable in Washington. The president's letter periodically reinforces these heavy responsibilities, and their attendant

---

* The "country team" is a State Department term for the standing committee of every American Embassy chaired by the ambassador and made up of the senior officers heading each section of the mission and the senior representatives of every non-State department, agency, and bureau having personnel in that embassy. The country team meets on a regular schedule, and/or when called together by the ambassador, to exchange information, to discuss policy issues, and to receive directives from the ambassador.

strong authorities across bureaucratic lines, and refreshes them for all to see the unique role of an ambassador.

Armed with these statutory and executive mandates, an ambassador inherits an embassy staffed with persons from two to several dozen agencies, from different cultures and with different focus. Taken together, the ambassador leads and manages government employees with interests and expertise that range across the spectrum of things important to Americans: population control, counter-narcotics, advancing America's economic interests, environmental issues, immigration issues and defense of our borders, human rights. Above all, the ambassador must keep in mind perhaps the most important aspect of having an overseas presence: ensuring the safety and welfare of Americans abroad. And all this must be done in a manner beneficial to the American taxpayer.

Beyond advancing national objectives, Motley points out, the ambassador must assume other roles in leading an American enclave overseas. An ambassador becomes the mayor of a small town, as American employees look to him for a variety of services they, as Americans, come to expect and as a government we should provide: safety, civilized living conditions, a reasonable education system for their children, access to adequate medical facilities and timely transportation modes to such, the anchor for American holidays like the Fourth of July and Thanksgiving.

To address all these issues within the context of the country to which he is assigned, the ambassador must mold and shape a mission statement for the embassy. A generic mission statement might include four main themes:

- Protection and welfare of American citizens
- Advancing the bilateral and global agenda of the United States
- Facilitation of U.S.business interests
- Stewardship of the taxpayers' resources

Key Ambassadorial Functions

One role of ambassadors underlies all of the others and will be vitally important in the years to come, notes Robert R. Bowie, a former Harvard professor and a top State Department official in past administrations.* The ambassador to a given country should be the primary source of intimate, in-depth understanding of the politics, economics, and social

---

* He served as assistant secretary for policy planning and as counselor of the State Department. His most recent publication, written with Richard Immerman, was *Waging Peace: How Eisenhower Shaped an Enduring Cold War Strategy,* Oxford University Press, 1998.

aspects of that country, and of its concepts of its national interests.

An effective foreign policy under conditions of global interdependence requires such understanding, both for forming ad hoc coalitions to cope with serious problems and for dealing with rogue or hostile states by intervention or other means of coercion. An ambassador and his embassy staff with genuine expertise on the ground can develop the necessary understanding and feed it into the policy process in Washington so that correct decisions and policies are arrived at.

Differing Roles in Different Countries

Frank Wisner, who served as ambassador to a number of countries in Asia and Africa important to the United States,* makes a distinction regarding the ambassador's role based on the country one is dealing with. The dominant factor in our relationship with Israel, for example, is the pursuit of the "peace process." Thus the policy conducted toward the Middle East, the peace process, is managed in the field by a special negotiator on behalf of the secretary of state and the president. That policy requires the involvement of a number of nations in the region and therefore is the responsibility as well of a variety of ambassadors, not just our ambassador to Israel.

In stark contrast to the U.S. ambassador in, say, India, the U.S. ambassador in Israel finds himself constricted in what he can do. The issues are of such moment that the National Security Council meets regularly to go over in detail each move that is taken. The special negotiator often operates with great stealth and in secrecy. The ambassador may not always be fully informed as to the state of play. So under these rather special circumstances, his role is more limited.

Public Understanding

Ambassadors must also play an increasing role in communicating with the American people, emphasizes former Ambassador Craig Johnstone.** No responsibility of the international affairs community is more important than establishing a dialogue with the American people on the appropriate international role for our country. Increasing congressional understanding of this essential role is equally important. If one were limited to citing one major deficiency in the conduct of foreign policy today, it

---

* These included Zambia, Egypt, Philippines, and India. He also served in Washington as under secretary of state and as deputy under secretary of defense.

** He served as ambassador to Algeria and in senior positions in the Department of State including director of resources, plans, and policy.

would be this one, he argues. The future of America is more and more tied to international events, but the people themselves are drifting toward indifference, protectionism, and isolationism, and Congress seems to be going along with this trend.

International news is covered less and less in local papers. Funding for the federal government's participation in international affairs is half of what it was in real dollars only a dozen years ago. Is it any wonder that popular support is lacking, given that public opinion polls show Americans believe we spend 15 to 20 percent of the federal budget on foreign aid, much more than we spend on Medicare or on our military forces? In fact, foreign aid accounts for a small fraction of 1 percent of the federal budget. Has there ever been an occasion in recent years when our president or other political leader gave a speech on television that made this point forcefully? Domestic political battles on completely unrelated issues have held up funding for international organizations, with which we lose influence with each passing year. Our overseas ambassadors, by virtue of their stature and access to the media, can aid greatly in correcting the misimpressions of the American people, Johnstone says.

The Role of the Embassy Staff

This book's emphasis on the roles of an American ambassador may give the false impression that he operates as a sort of sole practitioner in our diplomacy. The truth is that all ambassadors rely fundamentally on the men and women staffing their embassies to carry out all the functions assigned to that mission. Success depends on the quality of the ambassador's work, but without the essential contributions of his skilled and dedicated associates in the embassy he could not carry out his duties effectively.

But hereafter our focus will be on the roles of the ambassador. How he does his job, in a variety of foreign settings and under infinitely differing circumstances, is what this book attempts to show. It draws on the experiences of many American ambassadors, both Foreign Service officers and political appointees, who have filled these roles well, in small and big countries, in times of civil war or calm, in dramatic or quiet circumstances, and in headline stories and those that didn't make the news. It is a story about seizing the moment—sometimes in a dramatic way, but mostly in an everyday sense—while always dedicated to advancing the interests of the United States abroad.

Exercising Leadership

An American ambassador not only is our president's personal representative to the foreign government to which he is accredited but by tradition and by statute, and in some cases by consular treaties and conventions, is also the head of the American community in that country. The American community includes the U.S. government employees in or attached to the embassy—in large missions these officials can be from as many as 33 departments, agencies, and bureaus in Washington—resident American citizens, and transient or temporary American visitors. The residents might be businessmen, missionaries, scholars or researchers, journalists, relief workers, employees of international and multinational agencies, teachers, exchange students or professors, and dual nationals who are Americans as well as local citizens by virtue of marriage, original nationality prior to immigration to the United States, or naturalization.

Then there are the transient visitors. Predominantly tourists, they also include government officials—on occasion the president, the secretary of state, other cabinet officers, and members of delegations of the Senate and House of Representatives; sometimes governors and other state officials; and even mayors, seeking, for example, to develop trading relationships abroad. There are 101 reasons why Americans end up in a foreign country for longer or shorter visits. Every one of them looks to the American Embassy for various kinds of assistance, from arranging a meeting with the chief of state for our president to replacement of a tourist's lost or stolen American passport. The ambassador is ultimately responsible for all of these demands, though of course for most routine matters he relies on his staff of consular specialists. Many Americans, however, would be surprised to learn how often a "mere" consular matter requires the personal engagement of the senior diplomat present. Usually this involves some unwelcome incident or a lesser or greater catastrophe, which, from the point of view of the average citizen, would include loss of one's passport.

The Eyes and Ears of an Embassy

Unfortunately, because of budget stringencies imposed by Congress, and the reluctance of one administration after another to demand adequate funding for our diplomatic activities abroad, in recent decades America has closed many of its consular posts—consulates general in larger cities and consulates in smaller ones—forcing American citizens to rely in most countries on the embassy in the capital to provide for their needs. This is a surprising development, for one would think that our elected representatives would be especially sensitive to the needs of their constituents when they work or travel abroad. One justification for these closings is that the ease of modern travel, especially by air, makes it possible for Americans in need to get to the capital easily, quickly, and relatively cheaply, so one diplomatic post per country, the embassy, is all that is required.

What this argument neglects is that in large and important countries, say Germany, Britain, France, Italy, Japan, India, Russia, China, and Brazil, consular posts serve extremely important functions other than looking after American citizens. Most significant, they serve as the embassy's "eyes and ears" for understanding and reporting to the embassy on political and economic events, trends, and attitudes in provinces far removed from the capital. Ambassadors rely heavily on the information and analyses provided by these "constituent" posts to round out their knowledge of what is going on in the country at large. Imagine a foreign embassy in Washington trying to understand American society, politics, culture, and economics by relying solely on its contacts in Washington, with no input from New York, Los Angeles, Chicago, Atlanta, Seattle, Miami, Dallas, and Boston or even Des Moines, Omaha, and Charlotte.

Former Vice President Walter Mondale, who served as ambassador to Japan in the first Clinton administration, points to the critical contribution made by the five or so consular posts in Japan to his ability to carry out U.S. policies in that important country. He was able while there to add a small consulate in Nagoya and to resist pressure to close the post in Sapporo, a place that has a larger gross national product than France. Equally shortsighted, he says, "a costly, penny-saving mistake," was the decision he was unable to overrule that closed our small cultural office in Kyoto, the ancient imperial capital of Japan and today the center for practically all cultural events in Japan. "That office was closed, for budgetary reasons, on the same day that the newspapers were announcing that America had never been more prosperous." There was also pressure to close the Yokohama Advanced Japanese Language School that has trained so many of our Japanese-speaking career officers as well as diplomats from certain friendly countries such as New Zealand and Australia. Ambassador Mondale's leadership and influence slowed the contraction of the American presence in Japan, but the continued sharp decline in appropriations has been shrinking America's diplomatic and consular representation globally.

Looking After Our Citizens Abroad

Ambassador Mary Ryan, a career officer who has specialized in administration (that is, running embassies day by day for the more policy-oriented diplomats such as the ambassador, his deputy, and the political, economic, and consular counselors), is the assistant secretary of state for consular affairs in the State Department, a position she has held since May 1993.* She asserts that our government has no more important responsibility than the protection of its citizens abroad—the principal consular function. Indeed, consular work is a primary statutory requirement levied on the State Department and its overseas missions. Most Americans' only contact with our diplomatic and consular missions is when they seek assistance with consular matters. So this function is not something that can be avoided or downgraded. What is more, the impression created for American citizens in distress or trouble while abroad can form their entire attitude toward the federal government, a positive one if they are helped or a negative one if the services rendered are less than helpful, polite, and effective.

Ryan stresses that when consular work succeeds it is invariably because the chief of mission, the ambassador, takes a personal interest in seeing that that work is done well, that consular sections are inviting, clean, and well organized, with courteous staff, and because the ambassador intervenes personally in cases that call for high-level attention.

Warden Networks

Consular sections rely extensively on resident American citizens to assist them in a most important function. The so-called warden networks are staffed by private citizens who provide the means by which an embassy or consulate can notify all members of the American community of what is happening and what they should do during a local crisis or emergency, such as rioting, a terrorist incident, the breakdown of civil order, an earthquake, tornado, or flood, or any other disaster. The volunteer wardens are charged with notifying 10 or 20 or 30 other Americans of a particular problem and how the diplomatic mission wishes them to deal with it. The citizens receive no compensation and usually precious little recognition for this work.

---

*   She also served as ambassador to Swaziland.

Ryan cites the example of Ambassador William Swing, who served in Haiti during a particularly difficult recent period in that country's travails. Swing spent a lot of time with the local American wardens, invited them to his residence, and entertained them regularly. All that attention paid off handsomely when crises inevitably erupted.

He also spent his three-year tour in Haiti arranging for the renovation of the consular section of the embassy. The Consular Bureau recently asked the Disney Corporation, well known for its customer service, to examine the consular operations in Haiti and the Dominican Republic, the two halves of the island of Hispaniola. Though they are similar, the Dominican Republic is the more developed and sophisticated of the two.

Disney concluded that if your impression of the United States was based solely on a visit to our consular section in the Dominican Republic, you would think that the United States was dirty, disorganized, and rude. If, on the other hand, you visited the same place in Port-au-Prince, capital of Haiti, you would think quite the reverse, all because of the interest that Ambassador Swing took in making sure his consular section showed the best side of America.

Missionaries Assisted in Lesotho

It does not take a lot, Ryan says, to earn the gratitude of citizens who are assisted by an embassy's consular section, perhaps because Americans have low expectations of their government. As the assistant secretary in charge of consular work, she often receives thank-you letters from citizens who have been helped. A recent example concerned an incident in Lesotho, in southern Africa. An elderly missionary couple had been assaulted. The American ambassador, Katherine Peterson, dispatched her deputy to go to the missionaries' house as soon as she learned of the assault, at 3 o'clock in the morning. Ryan later received a letter from the American Baptist Society stating that never in their history had any official done that for their people, how impressed they were, and how their whole image of the State Department had been changed by the embassy's reaction to that incident. The leadership shown by the ambassador was of course crucial. CNN, Ambassador Ryan notes, reports incidents that happen overseas, but it doesn't do anything about them. It is not a substitute for embassies on the ground.

A Judge Rescued in Kenya

A dramatic yet not uncommon example of an embassy assisting a visiting American citizen in distress is recalled by career officer Elinor

Constable from her tour as ambassador to Kenya.* It concerns a distinguished American judge who was abducted in Nairobi in broad daylight.

Some people in the Kenyan government had come to believe that the Ku Klux Klan was trying to overthrow President Daniel arap Moi and that the Klan's representatives in the country were American missionaries. As a result the American missionaries had been expelled. In this setting, a retired American judge, Marvin Frankel, chairman of the board of the Lawyers Committee for Human Rights, had been invited to Kenya to observe a trial. He was accompanied to the court by a junior political officer from the embassy, who subsequently rushed into Constable's office breathlessly in the middle of the trial to report that the judge had disappeared.

"What do you mean?" she asked him.

"Well, Judge Frankel was sitting right there," he said. "I turned around, and suddenly he was gone. And I thought maybe he'd gone to the men's room, but he didn't come back. I asked around if anyone had seen what had happened, and someone had observed two goons come into the courtroom and escort the judge out, and he just disappeared."

Using the embassy's extensive local contacts, Constable learned that the judge had been carted off to a common jail cell. The jailers had taken his belt, his shoes, and so forth, and they were interrogating him about the Ku Klux Klan. They then transferred him to another building downtown, which was where the embassy finally located him. The ambassador dispatched the consul general to the building, but he was refused admission. So he started shouting, displaying a good deal of bravery: "I am here representing the American ambassador, and I'm here to rescue the judge." The Kenyans didn't know quite how to handle that.

Eventually he managed to get into the building and started wandering around looking for the judge. He saw someone being escorted across the end of a long corridor, and he shouted, "Are you the judge? I'm here to rescue you." He was able to take custody of the judge and took him straight to the airport, supplying him with some emergency toiletries. The consul general put him on the next flight to Europe and onward to the United States.

The judge made clear he wished never to set foot in Kenya again, but his opinion of the American Embassy was very high indeed. He wrote to Ambassador Constable when he was safely back home and said he

---

* She also served in Washington as assistant secretary of state for oceans and international environmental and scientific affairs.

was quite impressed about the speed with which the embassy had found him, rescued him, taken care of him, and sent him on his way home.

A Crisis of Leadership in Pakistan

Ambassador Robert Oakley* tells a tale of exercising leadership during a most difficult period, not so much for the nonofficial American community but for the official embassy community charged with managing our relations with the host government. It begins in August 1988, when he was working in the White House on the staff of the National Security Council, then headed by National Security Adviser Frank Carlucci and his deputy, General Colin Powell. Oakley was assistant to the president for the Middle East and South Asia, but his primary area of responsibility was Afghanistan and Pakistan, the latter country playing the important role of conduit supporting the war against the Soviet occupation of Afghanistan.

On August 17, 1988, the Pakistan Air Force C-130 carrying Pakistani President Zia al Haq and our ambassador to Pakistan, Arnold Raphel, crashed, killing all on board. General Zia had been Pakistan's all-powerful military and civilian chief for a decade, and although elections had been promised, there was no expectation of a new leader's taking office. Raphel was an exceptionally able and highly respected career diplomat. That evening Oakley and his wife, Phyllis, were having a sort of wake for Raphel at a Washington restaurant along with some of the late ambassador's close friends when Oakley received a phone call from Secretary of State George Shultz, who was in New Orleans attending the Republican National Convention. Shultz asked Oakley to be at Andrews Air Force Base the following day at noon, when they would take off with the delegation to attend the late President Zia's funeral. Shultz added that Oakley should "bring two suitcases because you will be staying behind as the new U.S. ambassador" to Pakistan.

The idea was to fill that post immediately, so that there would be no gap in representing the administration in Washington, with someone who knew the key issues in the relationship, had the necessary security clearances, and was well enough known by Pakistan, India, and the USSR. This was believed to be essential to help restore stability to a badly shaken and suddenly leaderless country suffering from understandable fears as to who was behind the plane crash (the USSR, India, Iran, inter-

---

* He served as ambassador to Zaire, Somalia, and Pakistan and in Washington as director of the State Department's Office for Combatting Terrorism.

nal enemies of Zia, and even the CIA were leading suspects). There was also a need to restore the morale of a badly shaken American Embassy, which was accustomed to Ambassador Raphel's strong leadership.

On the flight to Pakistan Secretary Shultz, Under Secretary Michael Armacost, Assistant Secretary of Defense Richard Armitage, and U.S. Central Command chief General George Crist decided upon strategy, objectives, and an approach to implementation. U.S. policy would be to focus on stability and a systematic strengthening of relations with the politically all-powerful Pakistani army. The objectives were to reassure the army of strong U.S. support against any external interference during the immediate crisis and over the long term, to maintain the army's support for the war in Afghanistan, to prevent the army from overreacting toward India, to not cross the Pressler Amendment's limits on Pakistan's nuclear program, and to allow the elections promised by Zia to proceed. This was a tall order for a shaken nation with no recent history of civilian, democratic government, but the delegation set about implementation with a series of meetings by Shultz with Pakistan's top military commanders and the new acting president, Ghulum Ishaq Khan (known as GIK), a highly respected civilian member of Zia's small inner circle and chairman of the senate. The secretary also met with the embassy staff to express sorrow over the loss of Ambassador Raphel, reassure them of his personal support, and formally introduce Oakley as the new ambassador. The paperwork for his appointment had been completed during the flight over, and he presented his credentials the following day, possibly a record for speed in installing a new ambassador.

The first order of business was to ascertain the cause of the plane crash to ease tension and allay suspicions. The U.S. Defense Department dispatched its best crash investigators, supplemented by security officers from the State Department. Oakley was able to persuade the acting president and Chief Air Marshal Hakimulla Khan to allow the Americans to join the Pakistani crash investigators and form a single team. They agreed to share all information and withhold nothing, on the condition that there would be no separate or interim U.S. report to Washington. Despite predictable pressure from Congress and the media, and similar pressures on the Pakistani side, the agreement held.

This helped immensely in establishing mutual confidence and paved the way for mutual acceptance of a split report: U.S. investigators found no evidence of an explosion or other sabotage and were confident that a faulty hydraulic system was responsible, as had been the case in several previous C-130 crashes. Nor was there any intelligence pointing to sabotage or terrorism, despite the many rumors. However, they stated there was no definitive evidence proving their thesis. The Pakistani investigators acknowledged that they had found no evidence of sabotage, had no evidence of a specific plot to cause the crash, and appreciated the thesis of the U.S. investigators, but were inclined to believe it had not been an accident. Both governments publicly accepted the conclusions of the report and did not question it privately, thereby getting over a difficult hurdle.

On the military front, the Defense Department pushed to the front of the pipeline Pakistan's pending orders for new F-16 aircraft, artillery, helicopters, and used naval vessels, and deliveries began almost at once. At the same time there were visits by the U.S. Army and Air Force chiefs of staff, Pakistan was assisted in planning its next major maneuvers (and persuaded to accept Indian observers), and its air force was helped in improving its performance against the Afghan and Soviet aircraft that periodically flew over Pakistan's territory. Pakistani officers were given priority slots in U.S. military schools, and there were joint field exercises and ship visits. All of this enabled Ambassador Oakley to gain the confidence of Pakistan's army chief to the point that they could discuss frankly the very tricky issues of elections and the nuclear program.

During the month of September it became clear that there was powerful opposition within the army and from Zia loyalists to the announced popular elections for a new parliament. Zia had done nothing to organize for such elections, whereas the Pakistan People's Party (PPP) had done a great deal. Led by the charismatic Benazir Bhutto, whose father had been deposed and executed by Zia, the PPP was likely to carry the day, with Bhutto becoming prime minister. The Zia loyalists set to work to create a coalition able to compete but wanted to wait until 1989 rather than go ahead with the November 1988 schedule. Others called for the old parliament, dissolved by Zia the previous spring, to be reinstated rather than have new elections. This would have created a major internal crisis.

Over a period of weeks Oakley discussed the situation at length with the acting president and the army chief, separately, urging them to pull the country together during a difficult, dangerous time by holding the scheduled elections, and thereby also generating increased support in the United States. Although the two top men were having difficulty talking to each other and making up their minds, and were being subjected to pressure from some military and intelligence circles, in the end they both decided to proceed with the elections.

Oakley was very careful not to have any direct contact with Bhutto or other candidates to avoid charges of interference. However, Bhutto had an enthusiastic, vocal group of supporters among U.S. Democrats, whose remarks complicated the embassy's efforts to keep the elections on course. Ultimately, reasonably free elections were held on time and certified by the United States and other governments, and the PPP did win a plurality and formed a majority coalition with Bhutto as prime minister. The army and acting president interposed no objections. They did, however, warn Bhutto before she took office not to interfere in security matters, including Afghanistan and the nuclear program. GIK was then elected president, sharing power in an uncertain constitutional relationship with her.

This was a great relief to Oakley personally and to the Bush administration and allowed the United States to proceed once again with certification under the Pressler Amendment. A strategy for certification had been worked out during the ambassador's visit to Washington in October, whereby both President Reagan and President-elect Bush (assuming he won) would provide Oakley with letters to President GIK and Prime Minister Bhutto stating that Pakistan's nuclear program was perilously close to the Pressler violation line and could not move another step or all economic and military assistance would halt.

The United States suspected but was not certain that Pakistan's program had crossed the line but decided to give it the benefit of the doubt—provided that elections were held freely and fairly and that there was no more nuclear movement. Given the prospect of seriously disrupting the war in Afghanistan should sanctions be imposed, this seemed the sensible course. Congress did not object, in part because key Democratic leaders on nonproliferation were also supporters of Bhutto. Oakley shared these letters with Chief of the Army Staff Aslam Beg and stressed the importance of maintaining U.S. military support. Beg visited the United States in January 1989 and talked privately with outgoing National Security Adviser Powell and his incoming successor, Brent Scowcroft, as well as others. Beg and GIK decided to hold back on further nuclear development (a decision that was reversed in the early 1990s).

By early 1989, only a few months after Oakley's arrival in Islamabad, the crisis had passed. Pakistan had a truly democratic government with a dynamic new prime minister (whose governance faltered badly over time), the USSR was preparing to leave Afghanistan, Pakistan's nuclear program seemed to be under control, and U.S.-Pakistani relations could hardly have been better. Oakley says that none of this would have been possible without an extraordinarily capable and cohesive embassy staff and dedicated and effective support from Washington.

Despite this book's emphasis on the role of the ambassador, all who have contributed to it would agree that when an embassy is working well it is because it is staffed by highly capable people who work hard, consider themselves members of a team, and enjoy excellent morale, as was the case in Islamabad as recalled by Ambassador Oakley. Fortunately for the American people, the Foreign Service of the United States is a well-trained and dedicated corps of professionals.

Management by Objectives

Ambassador Edward Rowell draws upon his tour in Bolivia from 1985 to 1988 to illustrate how an ambassador exercises leadership.* Thanks to the fact that the Senate was going through one of its periodic bouts of procrastination in confirming ambassadorial nominations, a phenomenon that has increased in frequency in recent years, Rowell had several months to prepare his leadership game plan for the embassy in La Paz. He used the time to get to know the principal actors in Washington concerned with Bolivia, to learn about the policy mandate he would have there, and to prepare himself to deal with the agency representatives who would be part of his staff in the embassy in La Paz, including a large number of law enforcement people who were likely to be unfamiliar with the normal strictures of diplomacy.

Rowell's Washington consultations led him to a very simple conclusion about U.S. policy. He was supposed to stop the cocaine trade in a country that had had more revolutions than years of existence. He was supposed to leave a democratic heritage in a country that had had a socialist revolution. And in a country that had nationalized large segments of its industry in 1952, he was supposed to engineer a market economy. His final instruction, he says, was that senior officials in Washington hoped they would not have to pay too much attention to Bolivia.

He took advantage of those long consultations to spend extra time interviewing people at other agencies with programs in Bolivia. The purpose was to create a sufficient "recognition factor" so that from the La Paz end he could pick up the telephone and talk directly with the head of the Drug Enforcement Administration (DEA) when he needed to.

---

*   He also served as ambassador to Portugal and Luxembourg.

Furthermore, he wished to be able to demonstrate that capability to the local representative of that agency on his staff in the La Paz embassy. One demonstration was normally sufficient to establish his authority as chief of mission.

He arrived in Bolivia and implemented his leadership strategy. It had four elements. The first was to exert substantive leadership, meaning he had to tell people what the policy was all about. The second was to show he was operationally engaged, so that the entire embassy staff could see that he knew what they were doing and that he would carry his share of the water when his intervention was needed. He emphasized his willingness to engage himself in their work, to raise issues with a host government cabinet member or even the presidency when that was important to advance the program of a U.S. agency in the embassy.

Third, he had to show his concern for members of the staff. And their families had to feel that the chief of mission cared about their welfare. Finally, the ambassador sought to demonstrate respect for each employee of the embassy and to show that he knew them as individuals.

Rowell says he had one more arrow in his quiver, but he didn't take it out for the first two months. It was to install what some would regard as an elaborate "management by objectives" system in the embassy. He went through the usual and absolutely necessary routine of calling on lots of people and establishing his official and personal relationships with the Bolivian authorities. He then launched the management by objectives program.

It consisted of three overall policy goals: eliminating coca, maintaining democracy, and creating a free-market economy. He chaired two long staff meetings with the country team to discuss his plan and then assigned the deputy chief of mission the job of directing the effort to devise seven major embassy objectives that would presumably lead to attaining the overall goals. Each section or agency was to prepare a work plan that would show what its specific objectives were. That included the DEA, the military attaché's office, the military assistance group, the CIA station, the aid agency, and other groups brought in later, such as the Border Patrol, the Coast Guard, and the Navy at one point (even though Bolivia is a landlocked country).

Once these objectives had been established, the ambassador tied the resource allocations to the system. For example, if there was "representation" money to be spent on entertaining someone or some group, it had to be tied to one of the specific objectives. Each section or agency was then required to establish a set of quarterly benchmarks. This reversed the usual way our government thinks, by looking at outputs, not inputs. The question is not how many lunches you bought but what you got in exchange for those lunches. It is not how many reports you wrote but what the reports did to help you meet the mission's objectives. Rather than focusing on the traditional reporting agenda, the political section was asked to report on how to get the Bolivian congress to pass the first-ever law to permit cutting down coca.

Rowell used the quarterly benchmarks, in reviews with each of the section and agency chiefs, to see how the embassy was doing. The process was a bit cumbersome at first, and some fears resulted from it. The section chiefs worried that they were going to be disciplined if they didn't achieve the objectives that had been laid out for them. That was a legitimate fear, Rowell admits, but once they understood that he was perfectly willing to change the time lines or to redefine certain of the benchmarks or objectives in the face of reality, they calmed down.

The purpose of this exercise was not merely to relate resources more closely to output but to get everyone to understand how they fit together, so that the political section, for instance, understood that the reporting it was doing was intended to help AID figure out which projects it should undertake and which ones it might need to cut back on. It was intended to make the air attaché understand that he had to post his flying schedule so that the political section could get out to the boondocks where there were no roads. It was intended to have the military figure out how to coordinate their inputs with the AID inputs, and with the DEA's activities, so that there was a reasonable synergy.

This exercise resulted in the embassy's taking a new policy initiative. At the end of three months Rowell called the country team together and declared: "All right, now let's review how we're doing on coca. Democracy is more or less going along. And the country realizes that with 23,000 percent inflation it will have to do something about the economy. So there is no need to motivate them in that area." The consensus was that the embassy wasn't really accomplishing much. It was looking good on paper in Washington, it was sending in telegrams saying how many times ministers and subministers had been exhorted, how many times business people had been talked to, and so forth. The coca was being cut down, but the street price kept dropping in Miami.

Rowell asked the group to focus on a specific problem area that could be addressed directly. The answer was the cocaine-producing laboratories located where nobody could reach them by road. What would it require to get there? Helicopters, of course. Rowell asked the Army attaché, a Vietnam helicopter pilot veteran, to put together an operational plan to bring in a U.S. Army helicopter battalion from Panama to fly the Bolivian antidrug police in raids on the laboratories. The attaché drew up the plan, Rowell made sure he coordinated with SouthCom in Panama, and then the ambassador submitted the plan to Washington on January 1, 1986. He did not hear back from the Department of State until June, when the response was: "Please obtain the Bolivian president's permission as soon as possible. We want to launch this attack plan in two weeks."

Leadership requires that the leader obtain allies in other agencies wherever he can. Fortunately, Rowell had a very good relationship with General Jack Galvin, the SouthCom commander in Panama, who kept him informed every step of the way about the helicopter project. USIA was asked to mount a special campaign to direct public attention to some of the terrible costs that cocaine production was inflicting on Bolivia's own society, and to point out how much we cared about ordinary peasants in Bolivia and how the programs the United States had underway would help ordinary people. The political section continued the effort to change Bolivian law.

The ambassador was of course responsible for dealing with Bolivia's president, with whom he had established a personal relationship. On receipt of the instruction from Washington, he arranged a private meeting with the president at his residence, with the result that permission was granted to bring in the helicopter battalion, the first operational deployment of a U.S. military force south of the Caribbean in this hemisphere, with the exception of U.S. Army Air Corps stations in northeastern Brazil during World War II.

The eventual outcome was that the operation cut down a lot of coca, thousands of hectares. But the farmers also moved farther out to more remote regions and started planting a lot of coca there. So it is not certain that much ground was gained in reducing production. But the new law that the embassy had sought was passed. Bolivian society was sensitized to the cost that the cocaine trade was inflicting on it, and there was a genuine turnaround in attitudes. A number of programs were initiated that helped to build ordinary people's faith in a market economy, including a small-loan program within the city of La Paz. Other programs were directed at villages around the country. By 1988 inflation had come down from 23,000 percent to 12 percent, and at one point it fell to 9 percent. There was an election that for the first time in Bolivia's history transferred power from one party to its opposition.

Washington wasn't as supportive of another of the La Paz embassy's initiatives as it was, albeit belatedly, of the helicopter project. Rowell and his staff came up with an idea about how to get the coca farmers to reduce their coca production. These were poor peasants. They had no shoes, no running water, no capital. And it takes two years to obtain a first harvest from a coca plant. The Bolivian government wanted to give peasants who stopped growing coca a $2,000 credit so they could survive for a couple of years until they put in an alternative crop. The embassy developed a plan for finding the money to finance the scheme.

Rowell traveled to Washington and managed to persuade every agency concerned, but he could not win the agreement of the deputy secretary of state, John Whitehead. Three times he "broke his lance on John Whitehead," as he puts it, trying to get him to approve the alternative crop scheme. In the end, the Bolivians found a source of funds that had nothing to do with the United States to start the program.

Policy Coordination in Washington

Edward Perkins, a career officer whose assignments included service as U.S. permanent representative to the United Nations,* is also a believer in management by objectives as the key to exercising leadership in foreign affairs and as a technique even more useful there than it is in the private sector. He points out that the foreign policy community in Washington is made up of a multitude of agencies besides the Department of State that have a partial interest in the totality of a given foreign policy issue. For example, the problem of developing operational policies for the sale of U.S.-grown wheat in overseas markets requires coordination in Washington and at certain posts abroad. The Department of Agriculture representing the farmer, the Department of Commerce representing the businessman, and the Treasury Department representing the effect on monetary policy all have a say in the matter. The Agency for International Development, the U.S. trade representative, the Department of State, and the National Security Council all have major interests as well.

---

* He also served as ambassador to Liberia, South Africa, and Australia and in Washington as director general of the Foreign Service. Ambassador Perkins was co-editor, with David L. Boren, of the book *Preparing America's Foreign Policy for the 21st Century*, University of Oklahoma Press, 1999.

A recommended policy—for example, providing subsidies to American farmers to permit them to sell their wheat at prices competitive with those of heavily subsidized European farmers—can be drawn up. But getting that policy decision to the president for signature requires sophisticated leadership, coordination, and management skills. Throughout the process—during formulation, adoption, and implementation—another set of players outside the executive branch becomes involved: Congress, local government, farmers, consumers, and advocacy groups. When the new policy is approved and reaches the ambassador abroad, he, ably assisted by his counselors, must manage its implementation while trying to ensure that we remain friends with the host government, the country, and its people. This phenomenon is increasing as issues take on multinational and regional dimensions in our globalized world.

Perkins emphasizes that foreign policy management would be diminished should the number of overseas missions and their staffing be reduced further. Many posts are understaffed now. Having adequate numbers of effective Foreign Service officers who understand foreign cultures intimately, who speak foreign languages fluently, and whose training and experience are irreplaceable, is critical to our foreign relations.

Policy Coordination in the Field

Ambassador James Blanchard, a former governor of Michigan, served in the first Clinton administration as ambassador to Canada. He and his staff at our embassy in Ottawa worked to achieve bilateral agreements on thorny issues, as described in chapter 3. As for the pervasive idea that most bilateral issues between different parts of the two governments could be handled by telephone, fax, or e-mail, Blanchard points out that there is no country in which it is more imperative to have an embassy, precisely because our relations need one overall coordinator and manager to keep the different parts of our own government from "free wheeling," working at cross-purposes, and confusing the host government about what our policies are. Furthermore, although a lot of people in Washington think they know a lot about Canada, that is not true, as evidenced by Washington's misreading (when Blanchard was ambassador) of the Canadian elections, of prospects for the North American Free Trade Agreement (NAFTA), and of the outcome of the Quebec referendum until set straight by the embassy, with the help of its consulates such as the one in Montreal.

It is a well-known fact, says Blanchard, that Washington can't handle more than three or four diplomatic crises at a time. Without embassies to keep track of the crises that are not being watched currently because they haven't bloomed yet, or are overshadowed by major events elsewhere, or are misunderstood as not really being crises at all, we would be caught napping more often than we actually are. Because of the major role that commerce plays in our relations with Canada—virtually every Fortune 500 company is involved with Canada—our embassy in Ottawa is called upon frequently to assist in resolving commercial problems. Our trade with Canada is greater than that with all of Europe combined, more than $1 billion a day, and it has grown by 59 percent since the signing of NAFTA. The potential for growth by small- and medium-size American companies doing business with Canada is enormous.

Ambassador Blanchard got involved in negotiations over wheat and beer and even in a big dispute over country music TV. But even more important was his role as coordinator of all our varied relationships with Canada. He points out that if one element of our relationship were to be left to its own devices and allowed to have its way excessively, that could jeopardize another element quite unrelated but very important on which we were trying to obtain Canadian cooperation. For example, our entertainment industry is very important to us, but if it got its way 100 percent in a dispute with Canada, it could undercut our ability to get Canada's agreement to participate in putting troops in Haiti or to maintain its peacekeepers in Bosnia, for example. Such matters can only be coordinated and balanced, with appropriate priorities assigned, by an ambassador and an embassy on the ground in Ottawa carrying out their understanding of our overall policy toward Canada as determined in Washington but implemented in the field.

When Policies and Goals Conflict

Ambassador Anthony Quainton, who has led embassies on three continents,* cites two areas in which ambassadorial leadership is difficult and far from routine. He refers to countries and situations in which the American people are not in agreement about what American policy ought to be, with a corresponding difference of views among the members of an embassy's staff and a lack of consensus on correct policy. Examples

---

* He served as ambassador to the Central African Republic, Nicaragua, Kuwait, and Peru and in Washington as assistant secretary of state for diplomatic security, director of the Office for Combatting Terrorism, and director general of the Foreign Service.

include Nicaragua in the 1980s, Vietnam in the 1970s, or South Africa in both decades. The local American community may also reflect divisions over policy, along with a tendency to be critical of whatever the government is trying to do, wanting it to be tougher or softer, more involved or more disengaged.

The challenge for an ambassador is to avoid taking a monolithic, brook-no-controversy-or-discussion approach to subordinates who may not agree with the policy being pursued but, rather, to encourage a reporting framework in which the widest possible set of views can be sent back to Washington. Such reporting can reflect both the good news and the bad news provided that it is accurate, soundly sourced, and devoid of personal bias. Quainton recalls, when he was ambassador to Nicaragua, being told by the White House that it didn't want to receive any more good news from Nicaragua because that wasn't helping the president. He says he was instructed to produce more bad news. He believes an ambassador has to allow his staff a certain amount of freedom to get the facts out as they see them, within some larger parameters set by the policy of the United States toward the country and the region where they are serving.

Ambassador Quainton's second point about leadership concerns the conflict that often occurs between an ambassador's wish to conduct a diplomacy of openness and access, to have his staff get out among the people, and to have an open door for the local populace, and the need to provide maximum security for our diplomats abroad and their embassies, which are under increasing threats from terrorism targeting both people and diplomatic premises. Our diplomats often disagree among themselves about where the emphasis should be put, about whether personnel should obey every letter of the security regulations or whether security concerns have become too dominant. Disagreements between ambassadors and their security officers are not unusual.

An ambassador wants to get the diplomatic job done, but by his own behavior in the area of security he sends a signal to the official community about how he rates the importance of observing security rules and guidance. To some degree Quainton faults his own performance as ambassador to Peru, where he fretted and chafed under the security rules imposed on him, including being accompanied by 14 guards wherever he went, day and night. He wonders if he set as good an example as he should have. He wanted to do his job in a certain way, and that is what he did. But the ambassador as leader must always be conscious of the example being set. There are no easy answers to this dilemma, he says, and it is true that there are some overzealous security officers and some undersecure ambassadors. This tension will remain a challenge for ambassadorial leadership.

Integrating Disparate Goals

Frank Wisner cites lessons from his time as ambassador to Egypt, a major partner in the Middle East peace process. There are substantial American interests and major forms of U.S. engagement in Egypt, and not only on the issue of peace in the region. During Wisner's tour, there were strategic access questions: the need to transit the Suez Canal or fly American aircraft through, the wish to maintain a strong military-to-military relationship supported by a billion-dollar-a-year military assistance program, and a program of large military exercises. There were the beginnings of a turnaround in the Egyptian economy, an opening up of that economy, and a need to reform the economy so that at a minimum there would be opportunities for American business but also a way to use the nearly billion dollars a year in U.S. economic assistance.

According to Ambassador Wisner, Washington never looked at Egypt as a whole. Washington did focus on how to pursue the peace process, on the conduct of the Gulf War and how to create an alliance with the Egyptians, and on how to secure the access we needed. But it fell to the ambassador to act as the integrator, to use the full array of tools available to reinforce the central strategic direction, which, at this turning point of our mutual history, was that Egypt should have a relationship with the United States that answered most of its strategic, defense, political, and economic needs. Since no set of instructions arrived from Washington that articulated a single overall policy toward Egypt, it was up to the ambassador to put all the elements together.

The same must be true, Wisner believes, for other major countries such as Russia, where the ambassador in Moscow is the point at which everything comes together: American business interests, the problems of our strategic arms relations, our political difficulties with the Russians over third areas, the assessments made to Washington of the domestic situation and where it is going, how to create the right context for visits and meetings between the top leaders. The ambassador there likely plays the same key integrating function that was required in Cairo.

The point is that policy doesn't always get synthesized at the Washington level because of the many different departments, agencies, and branches of government competing to get their point of view in the forefront or to prevail over others. Whereas at the other end, at the embassy in the foreign capital, there is only one ambassador, who represents everybody and everything, the entire American government, and he is able to pull all these strands together. At the embassy level the ambassador is the equivalent of the president in Washington, though Wisner is quick to point out that he does not have a command role. He is not a commander in chief whose word carries the same weight as that of a president or cabinet officer.

Integrating Law Enforcement Into the Embassy Team

When John Negroponte was ambassador to Mexico,* he dealt with the question of unilateralism as it relates to the law enforcement presence in our embassies. In Mexico 33 government agencies were represented in the embassy. There was a large law enforcement community: the Drug Enforcement Administration (DEA), the Immigration and Naturalization Service, the FBI, Customs, the Alcohol, Tobacco, and Firearms Bureau, the Federal Aviation Administration, and others. The DEA particularly had the notion that one could accomplish U.S. objectives more effectively through an activist operational approach rather than through a liaison relationship.

On the other hand, the ambassador believes that the FBI long ago learned that liaison was really the way to go, perhaps because of its experience during World War II, when the bureau stationed agents all over Latin America, something that gave it a larger body of experience working with foreign governments. Negroponte thinks this is a crucial issue for two reasons. First, it is not effective to be so operational as to border on the unilateral, as the DEA so often has been in the past. Second, in the 21st century, our ability to act unilaterally on the world scene in terms of our relative power vis-à-vis other countries is probably going to diminish. Thus, he believes, there will be a growing requirement for the United States to act in a more collaborative fashion.

Because of the many agencies operating in Mexico, Negroponte chaired a country team meeting every day attended by the heads of all the agencies. He limited the length to 30 minutes, but held it daily because he felt that he couldn't afford to be out of touch with any of those agencies. These were not pro forma meetings. Issues were discussed very candidly, and to his pleasant surprise, during the four-plus years of

---

* He served also as ambassador to Honduras and Philippines and in Washington as deputy national security adviser and as assistant secretary of state for oceans and international environmental and scientific affairs.

his Mexican tour, there were never any leaks or betrayals of confidence.

He found it useful to have officers of the Foreign Service work on issues involving law enforcement. A junior or middle grade officer in the political section had the full-time job of reporting on narcotics matters. He was not in the narcotics assistance unit but kept in daily touch with the law enforcement community in Mexico to understand what its members were doing and to report on meetings of the embassy's law enforcement committee. As a result, he succeeded in building a relationship of confidence at the working level with those agencies that turned out to be extremely useful to the ambassador and the rest of the mission.

An ambassador's opposition to unilateralism, and his promotion instead of cooperation and liaison arrangements over direct action by law enforcement agencies operating abroad, run the risk that he will be accused of suffering from "clientitis," a term of opprobrium that is shorthand for the accusation that an American diplomat is more sensitive to the wishes and concerns of the host government to which he is accredited than he is to the interests of his own government in Washington. This charge is routinely rejected by ambassadors, who insist that their only client is back in Washington but that their job is to represent that client in a way that will be most effective in the foreign environment. Critics of ambassadorial performance generally think that ambassadors are at their best when they act as messengers and simply advocate U.S. policies, deliver the message, and then take the heat if the foreign recipients don't like what they're told. Diplomacy at its best, however, is a matter of communication and conciliation, as well as of strong advocacy.

Influencing Policy At Home And Abroad

Under our Constitution the conduct of foreign relations is assigned to the executive power, to the president and officers whom he appoints, although certain aspects require the participation of Congress, particularly the Senate (in ratifying treaties or confirming ambassadors) and in some cases the whole Congress (in declaring war or providing appropriations to finance foreign relations activities). In fact the president establishes the foreign policies of his administration, although the number of officials who today participate in the process has grown enormously and includes vast numbers of parties beyond the Department of State and its Foreign Service. And a wise president does a lot of consulting with members of Congress of both parties if he wishes to avoid serious trouble.

Influencing Policy at Home

It remains true that foreign policies are determined in Washington and are implemented abroad by ambassadors who are presidential appointees and who receive their instructions from the president, the secretary of state, and their subordinates in the White House and State Department who are also presidential appointees. But one would be hard pressed to discover an American ambassador serving any modern president who simply sat back and waited to be told what to do without providing any input into the decision-making process.

The degree to which ambassadors attempt to influence the policies affecting the country to which they are accredited varies greatly and depends on many factors: their own personalities; their personal relationships with their bosses at home, if they have such; how strongly they feel that mistakes are being made, or opportunities being missed, in the bilateral relationship between the U.S. government and their host government; their willingness to engage in the intellectual and bureaucratic combat that may be required to change decisions reached or attitudes firmly held in Washington; the strength of their convictions and willingness to put their careers, or at least their tenures as ambassador, at risk to win the argument. It also depends a great deal, as we shall see, on the foreign nation one is dealing with.

India

India is a large nation that represents about 24 percent of all humankind. The very complex issues resulting from its strategic position on the Asian continent have overshadowed its bilateral relationship with the United States. In the mid-1990s, when Frank Wisner was ambassador to India, competing preoccupations of the Washington foreign policy leadership—the president, the secretary of state, the whole national security structure—meant that not much time was devoted to the management or oversight of America's relationship with India.

With the exception of some rather broad guidelines set out early in the Clinton administration as to how we should conduct certain policies, notably in the field of nuclear nonproliferation, Ambassador Wisner was given great latitude to define the approach to those policies, to articulate the policies in such a way that they would be accepted by Washington, and then to carry them out. He says he was rarely second-guessed. Occasionally he repeated himself to make sure he was being understood and sometimes modified his recommendations to meet a variety of concerns. He also had to exercise leadership to keep his country team—the representatives of the several agencies with personnel and programs at the post—working together in New Delhi so that they saw things the same way and could help bring along their agencies in Washington.

The essential problem in dealing with a country like India, where an overriding strategic context was lacking, was that each agency or set of policy interests had articulated over the years its own special approach. There were those who believed that the key to the relationship was nonproliferation—persuading the Indians to roll back or at least stop further development of nuclear weapons and missile systems. Others felt that India was a prime candidate as an emerging market and that the weight of our influence should be directed to commercial diplomacy, opening up markets to make American goods competitive in that marketplace. Still others believed that South Asia, India included, was a theme park for population concerns or refugee movements or drug trafficking. Wisner says that any ambassador in this situation enjoys a special responsibility. He alone, given the absence of a sustained Washington policy focus, can integrate these pieces within a political framework that provides the basis for sustained engagement with the foreign government.

Particularly in a case like India, a large and important nation, an ambassador is absolutely vital to help shape a consensus, Wisner argues.

He must define the elements of that consensus, give them a political context, lobby the agencies in Washington to adopt a given point of view, and then use his diplomatic skills to present the case in the best manner possible to the host government.

Most ambassadors assert that policies are determined in Washington, but that does not mean they cannot be influenced by the envoys serving abroad. If Washington is not much engaged with a certain country, Wisner suggests, it becomes the ambassador's responsibility to take the lead in setting policies and priorities.

An ambassador is given the privilege of being the first person, and sometimes the last person, who is listened to, whose influence in a set of decisions can be absolutely dominant, as long as he understands where critical players in Washington are coming from, how to relate to them, and how to address their concerns in the context of overall policy toward the host country. However tricky the situation is in a foreign country, no cabinet officer is likely to go in blindly and proceed on his own without taking advantage of the ambassador's judgment, assuming the ambassador is deemed to be a person who is astute and has established a record of credibility.

To be really effective in influencing policy, an ambassador must have a very good understanding of how Washington works, how bureaucracies interact, who the key players are, and what their agencies and departments are focused upon. An ambassador must also return to Washington regularly, as Wisner did during the course of his mission, to call on all of the principal actors. This enabled him to make sure that he maintained a consensus among the key players in Washington. From his posts in Cairo and New Delhi he made a practice of trying to get back to Washington once every six to nine months by whatever means in order to build that consensus.

Wisner regrets that congressional travel abroad has declined precipitously from what it used to be. Those visits by congressional delegations ("CODELS" in State Department jargon) help our legislative representatives educate themselves on the major issues and problems of foreign relations. In Egypt he received numerous CODEL visits, in India practically none. Some of the travel that still takes place is financed by interest groups that pay the costs when members of Congress want to go abroad. Wisner thinks it is not a good thing for senior public servants to inform themselves on behalf of their constituencies by accepting private funds to travel. They are traveling on official business and should use public funds.

Portugal

Senior career diplomat and cabinet officer Frank Carlucci* was U.S. ambassador in Lisbon in 1975, when post-revolutionary Portugal posed two starkly contrasting policy choices for the United States. The prevailing school of thought in Washington was that Portugal was all but lost to the Communists and should be isolated as a lesson to others who might be tempted to follow the same course. This was called "the inoculation theory." The other school, articulated by Stuart Scott, Carlucci's predecessor in Lisbon, was that Portugal was not irrevocably lost and that patient support was called for. Scott's advocacy of this view had caused him to be removed from his post and Carlucci to be rushed to Lisbon to replace him. Lawrence Eagleburger, then State's under secretary for management, had told Carlucci that the embassy in Lisbon was the most demoralized embassy in the world.

On his arrival Carlucci was greeted by an ideologically committed local press whose savage personal attacks were only somewhat attenuated by the grudging admission that he at least spoke Portuguese (he had served in Brazil). Daily demonstrations against the embassy were commonplace. At one point after an abortive coup attempt (with which the United States had no connection), the Portuguese general in charge of security went on television to announce that Ambassador Carlucci had been behind the effort and should therefore leave the country immediately. In effect, a bull's-eye had been painted on his chest.

On his first day in Lisbon, Carlucci had a meeting with Socialist Party leader Mario Soares, who could not have been more pessimistic. He said the prime minister, Vasco Gonçalves, was well known for his Communist views, and Communists controlled the key ministries, the press, the labor unions, and the top positions in the armed forces. Workers were taking over businesses, including foreign businesses, some of them American owned, and collective farms were being established on confiscated land.

Carlucci arrived in Portugal knowing little about that country and with practically no time to brief himself on it, but he was justly reputed to be a quick study. The United States was losing ground fast. It was time to take a deep breath and to think strategically. The liabilities were clear,

---

* In addition to his tour as ambassador to Portugal, Carlucci held the following positions in Washington in diverse administrations: deputy secretary and secretary of defense, national security adviser, deputy director of the Central Intelligence Agency, deputy secretary of the Department of Health, Education, and Welfare, deputy director of the Office of Management and Budget, and director of the Office of Economic Opportunity.

the assets less so. But as the ambassador reflected on the situation he decided there were some major assets. First came geography (Portugal was not aligned with any Communist country). Then there were the ties to NATO, economic links with the rest of Europe, and the conservative nature of the Portuguese people, particularly the small landowners in the north. Finally, there was the subtle but enormous influence of the church, notably at the village priest level. There was also the tendency on the part of the arrogant Communists to overplay their hand.

Conferring with his embassy colleagues, Carlucci decided that the key to exploiting these assets was to push for elections. As the embassy analyzed the prospects, the conclusion was that the democratic parties led by the largest non-Communist party, the Socialists, could win a fair election. The problem was how to persuade Washington to change its attitude. A lively exchange of telegrams did not produce the desired result, but the State Department did authorize Carlucci to return home to make his case in person. Washington was worried that the Communists could win, and there was also a visceral antipathy to the Socialists. The secretary of state had even called Soares—to his face—a "Kerensky" (the last pre-Communist leader of the Russian government in 1917).

Carlucci had two confrontational sessions with Secretary of State Henry Kissinger that did nothing to reconcile their views. The press reported that the secretary questioned Carlucci's "toughness." The ambassador, who knew his way around Washington extremely well, next relied on a very old friendship with Donald Rumsfeld, President Ford's chief of staff. This friendship, which began in their college years, had been solidified by their service together in domestic Washington agencies. After listening to Carlucci's pitch, Rumsfeld did not reveal his views and seemed to sympathize with the secretary of state. But the meeting must have had an effect, for the next time the ambassador met with Kissinger, the latter agreed to allow Carlucci to try out his policy recommendations and even offered his full backing for the change in approach.

The secretary's "capitulation" can probably be explained by his remark at the end of the meeting, when he told Carlucci: "The president wants to see you. What is that about?" No doubt the secretary preferred to effect a change in the policy approach to Portugal himself, rather than have the president order a change. Carlucci replied that he now saw no need for a meeting with the president. With good reason, Carlucci was known in the Foreign Service for being tough, resourceful, and persuasive in bureaucratic combat.

The ambassador used his time in Washington to put together a comprehensive program of assistance to Portugal based on elections and the anticipated triumph of the democratic parties. A housing program was already in the works. With his background in health care (as a former deputy secretary of health, education, and welfare), Carlucci started an emergency medical services program. He got the aid agency to establish a school of management at a local university. But the most critical need was to get the Portuguese military off the streets and back into their barracks. Something had to be done to restore their sense of pride and professionalism.

Carlucci flew to Brussels, to NATO headquarters, and enlisted the aid of Ambassador David Bruce and his deputy, Edward Streator, a college classmate of Carlucci's. Working with the senior military officer, General Alexander Haig, the group came up with the imaginative idea of creating a Portuguese NATO brigade. Carlucci helped draft the NATO telegram to Washington proposing this idea and then dashed back to Lisbon to transmit his own telegram endorsing the proposal. Washington liked the idea but lacked the money to fund it.

Carlucci next went to his colleagues in the White House Office of Management and Budget, where he had once worked. He obtained some funding there and got still more help from Senator Edward Brooke, a friend of Portugal on the crucial Appropriations Committee. Brooke arranged a hearing at which the ambassador persuaded Congress to finance a modest program of equipment, tanks, and armored personnel carriers for the Portuguese NATO brigade. The first M-113 APCs arrived in Portugal six months later and had the desired effect. The military professionals gradually gained the upper hand over the radicals.

The Socialists won the election. The problem then became giving them the means to straighten out the mess the country was in. Soares as prime minister promised to undo the nationalizations and restore property rights and the sanctity of contracts. In return he needed financial support. Carlucci and Soares developed a close relationship, getting in touch with each other four or five times a week.

Carlucci's next mission was to obtain a "jumbo" multinational loan for Portugal. Nine countries were to participate in a loan of $1.5 billion, a lot of money in those days. The United States had to take the lead, but the Treasury was initially opposed. Carlucci enlisted help at both the State Department and the White House and then overcame Treasury's opposition by having the Portuguese invite that department's under secretary to Lisbon. Portugal's new president, coached in advance by Carlucci on how to handle the visitor, carried the day. This was no doubt a curious way for an ambassador to deal with his own government, but not the first or the last time such a tactic has been used.

All of this gave the American Embassy in Lisbon enormous clout with the host government. The ambassador was consulted on virtually every major decision taken by the Portuguese. Carlucci and Soares became so close that the ambassador had to install a telephone at the embassy tennis court, because the prime minister liked to call him at precisely 5 p.m. every day, when Carlucci had his regular tennis game. They remain close to this day. (Not long ago Carlucci returned to Lisbon as a surprise guest to make a live TV presentation of an award to Soares as "Statesman of the Year." Carlucci's presence had been at Soares's request.)

Today Portugal is one of the world's success stories, a leader in the "third wave of democratization." It set the pace for Spain and the countries of Latin America. The Socialists were eventually replaced by the Social Democrats but then returned to power. The country, a member of the European Union, today enjoys a high growth rate, low inflation, and low unemployment. The embassy that Eagleburger had characterized as the most demoralized in the world became one of the best. It received an award for outstanding reporting, and a number of its key officers went on to become ambassadors themselves.

Carlucci draws several lessons from this experience. The most important is the most elementary. It is "know your host country," understand its people, and establish a personal relationship with its leaders. On arrival in Lisbon he set a goal of getting to know one new Portuguese leader every day. This kind of engagement can only take place on the ground, with a resident embassy, by an active and involved ambassador. It is the only way to obtain the knowledge and understanding needed to formulate a correct policy. Those who simply relied on press reports about the situation in Portugal were ready to write the place off. That would have been a grievous error.

Ambassadors must be policy players. In some cases they need to spend nearly as much time in Washington as at their post because Washington is where their problems may be. Had Carlucci not made his case personally in Washington on numerous occasions, his ideas would not have prevailed. In taking charge of a demoralized embassy an ambassador may want to try to do everything alone. A much better course is to provide good policy guidance, delegate lots of work, challenge senior officers on the staff to step up to their responsibilities, and reward good performance.

Finally, and perhaps obviously, Carlucci says one must have the courage of one's convictions. This may require career officers to make up their minds to resign if their recommendations do not prevail, something that happened to him twice. One of those times was in Portugal. But he did not have to resign.*

Philippines

Former Ambassador and Under Secretary of State Michael Armacost,** who now heads the Brookings Institution in Washington, was our ambassador in Manila when leading opposition figure Benigno S. Aquino Jr. was killed. Our abiding strategic interest in the Philippines was the retention of our military bases there. We also had an interest in promoting democracy. Under normal circumstances these issues were not as closely related as they became when the assassination disclosed the vulnerabilities of President Ferdinand Marcos and evoked a stronger than anticipated reaction among Americans and Filipinos for a restoration of democracy.

President Reagan, however, was a close personal friend of Marcos. In a way, the major contribution of the embassy, both during Armacost's tenure from 1982 to 1984, and perhaps even more importantly when Stephen Bosworth inherited those responsibilities, was successfully making the case that Marcos was the problem rather than the solution to the problem. Of course, that was not accomplished in a day but over a period of several years. First Armacost and then Bosworth systematically took advantage of every visitor to Manila, from Congress or the executive branch, to get that basic proposition accepted. They reinforced the point during their own visits to Washington.

Human Rights

Warren Zimmermann's contribution to this study concerns his work as head of the U.S. delegation to the review meeting of the Conference on Security and Cooperation in Europe (CSCE),*** held in Vienna from September 1986 to January 1989. (The name has since been changed to OSCE, with "Organization" replacing "Conference.")

---

* Editor's note: When I began my career as a Foreign Service Officer, my father, still serving as a career diplomat, gave me two bits of advice: (1) go wherever they send you and make the best of it—if you ask for a posting and you get it, you'll probably regret it; (2) never threaten to resign unless you mean it—your resignation will surely be accepted and you'll be out of a job.

** He served as ambassador to Japan and Philippines and in Washington as under secretary of state for political affairs.

*** He also served as ambassador to Yugoslavia and as director of the State Department's Bureau of Refugee Programs. His book, *Origins of a Catastrophe: Yugoslavia and Its Destroyers*, Random House, 1996, covers his service in that country.

The CSCE's membership was complex: all of the European countries except Albania, plus the United States and Canada. Its documents can only be described as dense and bureaucratic. Yet the CSCE played a major role in breaking down the barriers the Soviet Union and its allies had erected against free speech, freedom of movement, and open media, in opening the way to conventional arms control in Europe, and in increasing the pressures on Soviet leader Gorbachev for domestic reforms.

It was primarily a human rights forum, and as such it did not at first enjoy a high priority in Washington. In the 1970s, Secretary Kissinger had shown a negative interest in the human rights aspects of the organization, believing that our job vis-à-vis the Soviets was to change their international behavior, not how they dealt with their own citizens. Back then it had been the Western Europeans who had pushed the United States into the CSCE and into the Helsinki Final Act in 1975.

The CSCE operated primarily through review meetings, held every three or four years, that brought together large delegations from each of the 35 member countries to deal with such East-West issues as human rights, human contacts, freedom of information, economic cooperation, and arms control. Although the CSCE wasn't much noticed in the United States, it was viewed quite differently in Europe. For the Soviets it was actually a very important foreign policy issue. They liked to launch initiatives through the CSCE, such as grandiose arms control proposals, largely to obtain positions of influence in Western Europe.

But the tables were turned on them. After the signing of the Helsinki Final Act, dissidents in the Soviet Union and other parts of Eastern Europe began to quote back to the Soviets the language they had agreed to in the CSCE. And Helsinki monitoring groups were formed in the USSR and elsewhere. Solidarity in Poland was effectively a Helsinki monitoring group, and Charter 77 in Czechoslovakia also took its birth from the CSCE. These groups lobbied for the enactment of all the CSCE Helsinki obligations. However unimportant this conference may have seemed in the United States, in Eastern Europe and the Soviet Union it was enormously important.

To illustrate just how important the CSCE was to Europeans, Zimmermann cites two unusual experiences. As the meeting in Vienna began, Nobel laureate Andrei Sakharov was under house arrest in Gorki, a closed Soviet city. No one could visit him, certainly no Westerner. At Vienna the United States put a lot of pressure on the Soviets on the issue of Sakharov's detention, with the ultimate result that he was released from Gorki and allowed to return to Moscow. Zimmermann received a letter from Sakharov thanking him and stating that it was the work of the U.S. delegation in Vienna that got him freed. Zimmermann met another human rights hero, Vaclav Havel, for the first time at a CSCE anniversary in Paris in 1990. Havel thanked him personally, saying that the U.S. delegation at Vienna had helped the Velvet Revolution in Czechoslovakia enormously.

U.S. delegations to earlier review meetings were headed by very prominent Americans. For example, Justice Arthur Goldberg headed the first one in Belgrade, and Max Kampelman headed the second in Madrid. Zimmermann had been Kampelman's deputy at Madrid in 1980-81, and Kampelman had recommended Zimmermann to the State Department's European Bureau to be delegation head at the Vienna meeting. The bureau had been looking for someone politically prominent, someone with ties to high levels who could protect himself from attacks, for the CSCE had by then become a highly controversial affair. Reluctantly they accepted Kampelman's advice. Because Zimmermann had no lines into the presidency or clout with Congress, he had to work the bureaucracy to achieve success.

At the outset of the Vienna meeting in 1986, virtually no one thought it would succeed. In contrast to most multilateral negotiations, the policy issues at Vienna were highly complex. Covering the whole range of East-West relations, they were of great significance to the two great powers, to the members of NATO and the Warsaw Pact (particularly those Eastern European countries that used the CSCE to distance themselves from Moscow), and the neutral and nonaligned countries. By CSCE rules, nothing was decided until everything was decided, and every country had a veto—down to the last comma. A country as small as Malta could tie up a negotiation for weeks, which it occasionally did. Thus, the major issues at Vienna had to be resolved simultaneously. Arms control and human rights outcomes were inexorably linked.

This was early in Gorbachev's tenure in the USSR. He had not yet shown himself to be as flexible as he later became. The Russians fought every Western initiative on human rights. It became clear that the negotiations were going to last much longer than had originally been planned. Instead of six months to a year, they lasted more than two years. In the end the conference turned out to be a major success, the last significant achievement of the Reagan administration. The foremost historian of the CSCE process, William Korey, has written: "The results of Vienna in the human rights field were enormously impressive. Never before in [CSCE] history was so much progress realized."

Zimmermann says one reason for that success had nothing to do with the work of the U.S. delegation. It was the change in Gorbachev's attitude during the negotiations. The Soviet leader began to understand that he had to make some concessions to the West on the leading-edge human rights issues. The Russians moved from stonewalling at the beginning to allowing themselves to be dragged—often kicking and screaming—into concessions at the end that had earlier seemed beyond reach.

Such a positive outcome would not have occurred without a strong, clear, and consistent U.S. policy, which Zimmermann attributes to (1) a highly engaged secretary of state; (2) close coordination among the U.S. delegation, the State Department, and the other executive branch agencies; (3) a massive outreach to the human rights and (to a lesser extent) arms control communities in the United States; and (4) constant cooperation with Congress.

The complexities of the CSCE had been outside the attention spans of Secretary Shultz's four predecessors. Shultz took the Vienna meeting seriously. He was present at both the opening and the closing and learned the cutting-edge issues. Shultz always gave Zimmermann an audience whenever he returned to Washington from Vienna. Vienna became a key part of Shultz's meetings with Soviet Foreign Minister Eduard A. Shevardnadze and with his British, French, and German counterparts. When Shevardnadze surprised everyone at the opening of Vienna by proposing a human rights conference in Moscow, Shultz had an immediate and brilliant reaction. He told Zimmermann, "This is a better idea than the knee-jerk anti-Soviet lobby thinks. We can go along with it in the end, but let's make the Soviets pay for it if they want it so badly." That was the sort of guidance any negotiator prays for—knowing where you should end up two years hence and having the flexibility to plan how to get there.

According to Zimmermann, Shultz cared deeply about a good human rights outcome. He was the person who at the end had to decide that the negotiation had gone as far as it was going to go and that this was the time to cut a deal. No one else could have done that because any result was going to be controversial. At the time the deal was struck, some people thought the United States should have strived for a little bit more. But Shultz decided on the timing, and that was absolutely crucial.

The second reason for success was executive branch cooperation. Zimmermann's instructions were written in the European Bureau of the State Department, a powerful bureau whose voice was respected in

Washington. Two key individuals were involved: Rozanne Ridgway, the assistant secretary, and Avis Bohlen, the office director in charge of the Vienna negotiations. Zimmermann says they were remarkable, not only in understanding the complexities of this enormously complex negotiation but in providing the kind of backup that most negotiators can only dream about and almost never get. They fought the bureaucratic battles for the delegation in Vienna when Zimmermann couldn't return to fight them himself, and worked hard to win the support of the other agencies in Washington.

Ridgway and Bohlen were clear on the objectives, and they understood the problems. Their instructions gave Zimmermann both the authority he needed and the leeway he wanted. Not once was he micromanaged from Washington. In Vienna the U.S. delegation had representatives from the Office of the Secretary of Defense, the Joint Chiefs of Staff, the Arms Control and Disarmament Agency, the Department of Commerce, the CIA, and Congress, as well as staff from several State Department bureaus. After a few early mistakes, Zimmermann notes, he followed a policy of complete openness with the entire delegation, and it paid off—they became effective advocates to their own agencies on delegation positions.

Zimmermann's delegation was condemned to cooperating with another U.S. delegation, also in Vienna, conducting the MBFR (Mutual and Balanced Force Reductions) negotiations. The problem of coordination was serious, sometimes threatening the success of both negotiations, even though the two negotiations were entirely different. The CSCE was Europe-wide; the MBFR was between the two military blocs. The CSCE depended on the linkage of conventional arms control and human rights; the MBFR was devoted to conventional force reductions alone. Yet both negotiations had to conclude simultaneously and be consistent in substance. The CSCE delegation's nightmare was that the MBFR negotiations would delay or scuttle the CSCE negotiations; the MBFR negotiators feared that at the CSCE the United States would sell out Western security for the sake of mushy human rights objectives. Both delegations worked hard, and generally successfully, to overcome these differences. In the end, the last remaining difference—the timing of the endgame —was resolved by Secretary Shultz.

As the negotiations reached the final trade-offs, a familiar phenomenon appeared. Executive branch offices, which had not been paying close attention, woke up to the fact that irrevocable compromises were being made. This was particularly true of some staffers on the National Security Council, who all of a sudden voiced objections on a number of endgame decisions (including the Moscow human rights conference). There was the prospect that two years of painstaking work would go down the drain. Here again, the support of State's European Bureau and Secretary Shultz was critical. They wanted to end the negotiations; they had considered and approved the final compromises; and they had the bureaucratic clout to blow away the objections.

The third assist to a successful outcome was outreach to the non-governmental organizations (NGOs). This factor is unique to the CSCE experience, but it contains an important lesson: Anyone who is negotiating needs to pay attention to the political base at home on the issue being dealt with and to make sure those people and organizations are supportive. One of the unusual characteristics of the CSCE was the degree to which NGOs made a direct contribution. In the United States, human rights NGOs were consulted on positions the delegation should take. Their guaranteed presence at CSCE meetings was a major Western position—and a contentious one with the Soviets. Zimmermann took 20 NGO representatives to Vienna as public members of his delegation, and he scheduled multiple briefings of NGOs in Washington and around the country during breaks in the negotiations.

Non-governmental groups live with the suffering of human rights victims. They attract committed, passionate people to their cause. They are naturally suspicious of government officials entrusted to deal with human rights, and they do not like compromises that leave some victims unattended. As the head of the delegation, Zimmermann was the person they sought out. He had to convince them that the official delegation shared their commitment to a positive human rights result and that any compromise would be the best possible deal that could be obtained. In his briefings of NGOs he tried to get them to view the negotiations through the eyes of a negotiator, to see the problems as well as the possibilities, and to understand that achieving good results is better than chasing impossible perfect ones. This effort proved valuable. When the outcome was achieved, the NGOs led the cheering for it.

Lastly, the CSCE was unique in U.S. diplomacy in that our participation was authorized by statute and was a joint undertaking of the executive branch and Congress. Legislation in the 1970s created a joint CSCE Commission of Congress, with members from both houses and from the executive branch (the State Department member is the assistant secretary for human rights and humanitarian affairs) and with a broad mandate in the human rights area. The commission has traditionally helped to staff CSCE meetings. At Vienna one of Zimmermann's two deputies was the commission's staff director, and roughly a third of the delegation members were commission staffers.

The commission had been launched in a sea of bad blood. The secretary of state at the time, Kissinger, had tried to prevent its creation, and suspicion lingered among the commission members and staff involved in that early skirmishing. The commission gave Congress a quasi-executive role, and it was very jealous of its prerogatives. That was precisely the reason Secretary Kissinger had tried to prevent its creation. He thought it violated the separation of powers under our Constitution, and to a degree it certainly does.

The commission's hybrid nature threatened to create serious problems. On the one hand, as part of the U.S. delegation, it was subject to executive branch discipline. On the other, as an organ of Congress it felt free to criticize—publicly as well as privately—the delegation's work. As chief negotiator, Zimmermann decided to treat the commission staffers in Vienna exactly as he treated the executive branch people, believing that their competence, character, and loyalty would protect the negotiations from the inevitable sniping from Capitol Hill. The attacks that came from Washington during the endgame—that too much was being given away, that the U.S. delegation was rushing to a bad result—turned out to be short-lived, thanks largely to the commission teammates who knew better and said so. Zimmermann cites the late Ambassador Sam Wise (former FSO, commission staff director, and deputy head of the U.S. delegation) for his advocacy with the commission members, and Senator Dennis DeConcini and Representative Steny Hoyer for being especially farsighted in overcoming their earlier objections and supporting the final result. In the end the Vienna meeting marked a milestone in the human rights progress of millions of people who had suffered under Soviet control or influence.

Influencing Policy Abroad

The essence of diplomacy is communication. Leaving multilateral diplomacy aside, it is the sending and receiving of messages bilaterally between the governments of sovereign nations to harmonize their interests, to maintain and, if possible, improve relations, to avoid or ameliorate conflicts (most of all wars), to create alliances against potential enemies, to promote mutually beneficial trade, and to discover potential areas of cooperation that will advance the interests of both nations. Ambassadors who simply deliver messages on these matters, and receive replies to be transmitted to Washington, are not doing their jobs. All such messages have contexts and antecedents that require explanations and need to be interpreted, or they risk being seriously misunderstood with possibly dire consequences, especially if they are not entirely friendly. An ambassador who acts as a mere messenger is not a competent diplomat.

United Kingdom

Historically our most important diplomatic mission has been the one in London, its presence there now dating back nearly 215 years. The only break in its existence came in 1812-15, when our two countries were at war. It is our only diplomatic mission that had never been headed by a career diplomat until the appointment of Raymond G. H. Seitz in 1991.*
He was uniquely qualified for that position: In the 1970s, after having served at several posts in Africa, he became the "Africa watcher" in the political section of the embassy in London; in the 1980s he served as the deputy chief of mission in London, with the rank of minister, under Ambassador Charles Price; and from 1989 to 1991 he was the assistant secretary of state for Europe in Washington, a job that of course included oversight over the London embassy. President Bush appointed him as ambassador in London, and he continued in that post into the early years of the first Clinton administration, until mid-1994.

With his long service in London Seitz not only had a superb under-standing of British politics, economics, culture, and history but had amassed an exceptionally large and wide set of personal relationships with the British leadership in practically all walks of life. These are the elements that, when combined with the diplomatic skills honed by decades of service abroad and at home, make for a first-class envoy.

There exists a myth about our diplomatic relations with Great Britain that goes like this: If an issue of supreme importance arises, our president calls the British prime minister and they sort the problem out. If it is of lesser magnitude, our secretary of state phones the British foreign secretary and they agree on how to proceed. Thus our ambassador in London is relegated to participating in ribbon-cutting ceremonies, making speeches to business associations and academic audiences, attending receptions, luncheons, and dinners hosted by self-important or social-climbing personalities, and perhaps enjoying some fox hunting with members of the aristocracy.

---

* In Washington he served as assistant secretary of state for European affairs and as executive assistant to the secretary of state. His account of his stewardship of the American Embassy in London is recorded in his book entitled *Over Here*, Trafalgar Square, 1998.

Ambassador Seitz of course strongly disagrees with this view, which he describes as people thinking that our ambassadors are really running branches of American Express abroad. Conversely, he stresses the role of the ambassador as both the public and the private voice of the U.S. government in the country of his assignment. While he doesn't make the policy, he can influence it in major ways. But he is the person who presents it to the host government. He receives an instruction to say something to the foreign secretary or the trade minister, to explain an American official policy, but he doesn't just read the thing out loud. He puts it in context.

To do this effectively an ambassador must know his own government and how it works. He can then explain to his foreign interlocutor where and why a policy originated, what the pressures on the president or the secretary of state are, what the constraints Washington is operating within are, whether there are congressional aspects, and so forth. In the same manner an ambassador, in reporting the host government's reactions back to Washington, must have the ability to explain the local political context to Washington. What are the pressures that the prime minister is under on this particular issue? Are there ways we can help that leader deal with those pressures so that he can decide to do what we want?

In that case the ambassador is the private voice. But he is also the public voice, and not only when making speeches. When we are dealing with democratic nations, the people want to know, to understand, to have things explained to them. So the ambassador has to be able to stand up in front of a camera, or sit down behind a microphone, and explain to the public or the media, in as forthright a manner as possible, why the United States "is going bananas over bananas," for example. The ambassador may not be convincing, but at least he has had an opportunity to make a case.

"Part of that," Seitz says, "is kind of British. The British would say, 'There go those Americans again,' but often it wasn't a case of there go those Americans again." He cites an instance during a round of GATT talks in which the American position on the issue was being misreported in the British newspapers, and he knew there were going to be a lot of editorials the following day that would get it all wrong. The media simply did not understand what the U.S. position was and why we had done what we had done. So, using his good contacts in the British press, Seitz phoned editors at the *Times*, the *Telegraph*, the *Express*, and another paper and explained the issue to them. First, they were immensely appreciative of receiving his explanation. Second, the next day they published very good editorials. Third, the only way this could have worked was if the ambassador had known the four editors personally and had their trust. Only an ambassador on the scene could have had that kind of instant access, nurtured over a period of time, and a reputation for straight talking and being worth listening to.

In other situations the ambassador serves as a sort of punching bag to help defuse anger and aggravation. Of necessity Seitz played that role when the Clinton administration overruled the advice of the State Department, the Justice Department, the CIA, and certainly the view of our embassy in London and ordered the issuance of a visa to Gerry Adams, the leader of Sinn Fein, the political arm of the IRA in Northern Ireland. That gesture set off angry reactions in the British government, to put it mildly. It was personally insulting to the prime minister. Parliament was up in arms. The press was intensely critical. The British public was aroused. For Seitz it was the most uncomfortable period of his career.

He permitted himself to be "used." He was summoned to see the prime minister and was chewed out. Of course, he had to meet with the press and try to explain what his president was doing. This was extremely difficult for him to do because he was utterly opposed to the decision. But in such a situation the job of an ambassador is what is known as damage control.

Seitz makes the point that the American government is very fragmented. We have a peculiar way of governing ourselves that puzzles foreigners a great deal. We like our system because it's very democratic, but it's often inefficient and confusing, with many competing executive departments and agencies, a White House managing the politics, the lack of a cabinet structure for decision making, and all the congressional interests. This is not something that is ever going to be corrected, and perhaps it shouldn't be, but it makes understanding the nature of our own government a fundamental requirement for an ambassador to be effective in the field. A very good grounding in how Washington works is essential for an ambassador. Without it he cannot explain a lot of things to his hosts.

This is not an easy education to acquire. Service in the U.S. government or long involvement with it is an asset for any diplomat. Seitz, for example, had the advantage of having been in senior positions in Washington, as executive assistant to Secretary of State Shultz and as assistant secretary for Europe. When he worked for Shultz, he says, the latter spent 80 percent of his time struggling with his own government, dealing with the Defense Department, the National Security Council, the CIA, and Congress —he was engaged in an internal battle when he was supposed to be dealing with external, that is, foreign affairs.

At one point in London, during the Gulf War, there arose the issue of "friendly fire," of whether the American military were responsible for the deaths of some British soldiers. The American Embassy was doing all the proper things, reporting local concern and making recommendations on how to handle the problem, but it was extremely helpful to Seitz to be able to pick up the phone and call General Colin Powell, a former colleague in the Washington policy-making establishment, for a personal briefing on the situation.

The personal relationships he developed during service in Washington were a great advantage to Seitz in London for his dealings with the Joint Chiefs of Staff, the National Security Council, and the president and cabinet officers at a time that coincided with major changes in Eastern Europe, the reunification of Germany, the transformations in the Soviet Union, and the Gulf War. He was not inhibited from picking up the telephone and calling someone in a key position in our government whom he knew personally.

An ambassador heading an embassy abroad has an advantage unknown in the Washington bureaucracy. He not only controls (although sometimes not as much as he should be able to) the communications that travel from his embassy to Washington, but he can send personal messages, ordinarily by telegram, to his bosses in Washington, without having to clear them with (that is, obtain the concurrence of) anyone else on his staff. That is not how Washington works. To get an instruction sent out of Washington to an embassy, the clearances—required to be obtained from practically anyone who has an interest in the issue, or can pretend to have one—not only provoke interminable bureaucratic combat but can transform and dilute the message until it is a candidate for the lowest common denominator of policy.

On the other hand, it is truly amazing how well a message from an ambassador is usually received and how effective it can be. All he needs to do is put a high classification on it, like "secret" or better, and label it "NODIS," which means "No Distribution" but in fact ensures its distribution to the most senior policy officials in the U.S. government—and a demand by people who are not included in the initial distribution that they be allowed to read it. As Seitz says, such designations cause "the value of the currency to rise."

He offers two examples. He was working for Shultz during the Lebanon crisis. It was an everyday preoccupation, the government was "all over the place," and decision making was terribly difficult. But when a diplomatic telegram arrived from career officer Philip Habib, the special negotiator for the crisis in Lebanon, "everyone would gather around and read that telegram and discuss it. And it would not only influence the thinking, it would help the decision making." Habib was playing the role of an ambassador, reporting from the field without having to clear his advice with anyone, and with the massive amount of information available, Habib's advice was vital; it "was where it all came together," where one person, on the scene, gives advice that is the best informed and argued, and cannot be ignored.

Recalling when he was assistant secretary for Europe, Seitz says, "When Jack Matlock sent in a telegram from Moscow saying this is how it is here, this is what is going on, everybody read that telegram. It didn't even have to be NODIS. That telegram suddenly became the agenda item for the next meeting chaired by the secretary. If he's smart the ambassador will draw on all the expertise of his staff, but he doesn't have to clear it with them. This is the ambassador speaking. He signs the telegram and it is his view. He can speak to all of Washington, and they listen, and I've seen it often—it has a tremendous impact."

It's a bit ironic that a NODIS telegram obtains the widest distribution at senior levels and has the greatest impact. Asked to explain this phenomenon, Seitz says: "It's a Washington game. It doesn't matter what it says. If you give it that label—it doesn't even have to be sensitive—you get to say at the top of it how you want it distributed. I want this sent to the Joint Chiefs of Staff. I want it sent to the national security adviser. He'll see to it that the president reads it. Don't worry: The CIA will get it."

Maybe the ambassador even hopes someone will leak the telegram to Capitol Hill. And then the word gets around town, and everybody else wants to see it. An ambitious ambassador perhaps hopes that his brilliant telegram will attain the status of George Kennan's famous "long telegram" from Moscow that established the containment policy toward the Soviet Union and its budding Communist empire right after World War II. Something of that magnitude may happen only once in a generation, but it keeps hope alive for diplomats that they may actually have an impact on a major American foreign policy. That hope is sometimes their only reward.

Japan

In 1989 Michael Armacost was the ambassador in Tokyo* when the United States attempted a negotiation that was without precedent. The structural impediment negotiations were aimed at addressing underlying issues that affected trade but would normally not be part of a bilateral negotiation between governments. For example, the level of a country's savings/investment balance, its distribution system, and its antitrust laws seemed pretty delicate, and close to the bone of sovereignty, to take up in bilateral negotiations. The embassy did not propose these negotiations. Its role was more in shaping an idea that came out of Washington—to try to make it more palatable to the host government, and thus diminish the likelihood of provoking a nationalist reaction that would impede negotiations and complicate the management of other aspects of the bilateral relationship. The embassy argued that it should be presented as a negotiation in which both sides could raise their structural issues, that is, to make it a two-way street.

The embassy devoted a lot of its reporting to putting forward a menu of reform possibilities that had been authored by the Japanese, either by academics or by reform commissions of one kind or another. Our delegation could use ideas that did not have a "Made in the USA" stamp on them, thereby making it more difficult for the Japanese to toss them out as alien or inappropriate. The embassy also proposed going on the offensive in a proactive way, suggesting that the delegation explain the purpose of the U.S. proposals in public, underlining the benefits they could bring to Japanese consumer interests, and in some cases producer interests in Japan itself. In sum, the embassy exerted influence in shaping the implementation of an idea that had basically germinated in Washington.

Canada

If there is one country where it could be argued that we have no need for an embassy, it would be Canada. Our two nations enjoy probably the longest uncontested, undefended border on the globe, and we are each other's major trading partner, are allies in NATO, have cultures that are similar though not identical, are both nations largely of immigrants, and share a common majority language. When there are bilateral issues to resolve, it seems the senior officials of the relevant departments and agencies in the two governments could simply get on the phone and

---

* His book covering his service in Japan is entitled *Friends or Rivals?*, Columbia University Press, 1996.

together work things out. That is a utopian view, however, given the history of issues such as fisheries competition, environmental concerns, law enforcement cooperation, relations with Cuba, and Canadian concern about cultural dominance by the United States, to name a few.

President Clinton in his first term appointed former Michigan Governor James Blanchard ambassador to Canada. The major issue at that time was negotiating NAFTA (the North American Free Trade Agreement) with both Canada and Mexico. In January 1994, once the trade agreement with Canada had been secured, Blanchard turned his attention to another glaring issue that he hoped to solve as a memorable achievement of his tour in Ottawa. This problem had been bothering him because he had been experiencing it repeatedly himself. He described the situation in his book about his time in Ottawa:*

There was, for instance, the awful propeller plane between Ottawa and Boston. It looked smaller than the one used in "Casablanca," was jam-packed with thirty-three people, and reeked of the lavatory. There was the other old prop between Washington and Montreal via Philadelphia, in which the passengers were treated as though they were either deportees, forced to leave the United States under duress, or refugees desperate to get to Canada by any means at all. Then there was the five-and-a-half-hour marathon between our two great capitals: 9:00 a.m., depart from Ottawa to Toronto; 9:55 a.m., arrive Toronto, change terminals, transfer luggage, clear customs; 11:00 a.m., depart Toronto; 12:15 p.m., arrive Boston; 1:10 p.m., depart Boston; 2:35 p.m., arrive Washington and put in claim for missing luggage. Each and every one of these flights was a painful testimony to Air Canada's grip on the government of Canada. Neither the bureaucracies of our two countries, nor the politicians apparently, had realized what a modern transportation system could actually do for people and commerce.

Another time, en route from Washington to Ottawa via Pittsburgh, Janet and I saw people turned away from the plane even though there were six empty seats. "The reason," the pilot announced from the cockpit, "is due to the bilateral aviation agreement between the United States and Canada. We're only allowed to have a certain number of passengers on this plane. If we filled

---

*   *Behind the Embassy Door: Canada, Clinton, and Quebec.* McClelland & Stewart, 1998. Quoted by permission.

those seats, not only would the United States run afoul of the agreement, but this airline's access to the bilateral would be jeopardized."

All aviation relationships between countries are governed by a bilateral treaty or agreement that regulates the carriers and number of flights in and out. The United States and Canada had one of the longest and most extensive aviation relationships in the world, of course, but they were operating under an outmoded, highly restrictive regime. Thirteen rounds of negotiations had failed to significantly update it in two decades. There had been three attempts within the past ten years, and both sides had totally given up trying.

Ambassador Blanchard set as his personal goal the conclusion of a new, modern, sensible, mutually beneficial bilateral aviation agreement. Everyone counseled him that it couldn't be done, and they were nearly right. The problem was that the bureaucrats on the Canadian side were firmly entrenched and were opposed to any changes. What Blanchard strived for was an "open skies" agreement with Canada like the ones we were negotiating with the United Kingdom and Germany, both of which had higher priorities in Washington's eyes. But the State and Transportation departments encouraged Blanchard to try his hand in Ottawa.

He set to work with his deputy, economic minister-counselor, and other staff members and spent part of every day working up a new framework for an agreement. The goal was to institute a policy that would allow any American or Canadian airline to fly international flights into any American or Canadian airport. Later, perhaps, that could be extended to domestic flights as well. Previously, the American officials had despaired of getting a new deal with Canada, and they were facing Canadian officials who feared that any change would harm the two major Canadian airlines (one of which had been 100 percent government owned until 1989) and somehow compromise Canadian sovereignty.

There were no scheduled flights from Ottawa to Chicago, let alone Washington, none from Vancouver to New York, none from Montreal to Miami, and only three nonstop flights from Halifax to the United States. Two-thirds of the existing flights were operated by U.S. airlines, primarily USAir, Delta, and Northwest. Two-thirds of the remaining third were operated by state-owned Air Canada. And two-thirds of all the major airport cities in both the United States and Canada had no nonstop service between the two countries. The relevant cabinet officers in both governments eventually agreed to negotiations, and special negotiators were appointed, but the entrenched bureaucrats were successful in sabotaging a meeting of minds. Only the embassy in Ottawa was working this problem on a daily basis, as the bureaucrats in both capitals seemed to have other preoccupations. Without constant prodding from the ambassador and his embassy, the negotiations would have stalled, as they always had in the past.

Blanchard went on the offensive and gave speeches throughout Canada, using "public diplomacy" to lobby for popular support for change. He used a favorite comparison that always drew laughter but drove home the absurdity of the current, outmoded agreement: "What's the difference between the Ottawa International Airport and the White House lawn in Washington? Well, planes land on the White House lawn," a reference to a bizarre occurrence then in the news. The Ottawa Airport provided very little service, which everybody in the Canadian capital was irate about. This was not the behavior usually expected of an American envoy, but it was effective. He was, after all, campaigning publicly on Canadian soil for a change in Canadian policy.

It took about a year and a half, but an open-skies agreement was finally drawn up. A visit to Ottawa by the American president scheduled for February 1995 was to provide the catalyst to get the deal actually signed. Just before Christmas the two sides had agreed on the text of a joint announcement of the agreement. But suddenly another issue emerged that threatened to submerge the news. Canada was proposing to impose a new tax on American magazines as part of what came to be known as the "culture war" between the two countries. Fearful that the open-skies announcement would be blown off the front pages, Ambassador Blanchard phoned journalists at the five key Canadian media outlets and gave them a "confidential exclusive" on the forthcoming aviation agreement but embargoed it until a day later. The idea was to allow the reporters to get their stories ready in advance and "in the can" so that they wouldn't be trumped by the magazine tax story.

The inevitable happened. The next morning a friend complimented the ambassador on the "great stories in the papers about this new open-skies stuff." The reporters had violated the embargo and had attributed their stories to Blanchard by name or to "a senior U.S. government official." This unauthorized leak caused a furious Canadian side to threaten to cancel the deal, but a counterthreat by the American side to make the agreed-upon announcement unilaterally turned back the tide. The last-minute attempt by the Canadian bureaucrats to stall the announcement in the hope of killing the deal was thus thwarted, and the leak actually helped by bringing it all into the open.

The agreement was signed during President Clinton's visit. To quote again from Ambassador Blanchard's book:

Within the next three years, U.S.-Canada passenger traffic increased 37 percent, over forty new pairs of cities received direct service for the first time, and traffic levels between many old markets such as Toronto-New York or Vancouver-Los Angeles increased dramatically. The number of passenger seats per year between our two countries increased by 3.5 million. The combined net economic gain for both countries in activity and jobs was estimated in the billions of dollars, and all the airlines entered into creative joint ventures that resulted in better customer service and higher company profits.

All of this would not have been achieved without the work of Ambassador Blanchard and his staff at our embassy in Ottawa.

Mexico

From 1989 to 1993, when John Negroponte was our ambassador in Mexico City, the United States had two overriding issues in regard to Mexico. One was the commercial relationship, and the free-trade agreement (NAFTA), which was negotiated and concluded during his time in Mexico. That very important agreement moved along nicely on its own track, although other irritants in the bilateral relationship at times threatened to derail the process but never quite did.

The second major issue, one that took much more of the ambassador's personal time and involvement, was the effort to combat the illicit narcotics traffic originating in South America, transiting Mexican territory, and reaching the United States. The most amazing aspect of this issue, which Negroponte could hardly have anticipated, was that one incident so affected the overall relationship—the 1990 kidnapping of a doctor named Humberto Alvarez Machain, who was suspected of having been involved in the torturing and killing of a DEA agent named Enrique Camarena in Guadalajara in 1985. Alvarez Machain was accused of having used his medical skills to keep Camarena alive while he was being tortured. The Mexican doctor was kidnapped from his office by bounty hunters in the pay, ultimately, of the U.S. Drug Enforcement Administration. He was taken across the border to El Paso, Texas, and held under U.S. jurisdiction until he was tried several years later and, somewhat ironically, acquitted for lack of sufficient evidence. But this episode poisoned the atmosphere between Mexico and the United States for years. For the embassy in Mexico City it was a problem of limiting the damage and managing the issue. For Mexico it was a question of sovereignty, as it would be for any country, but particularly for a neighbor sensitive about its relations with the United States on a neuralgic issue. For Negroponte it was probably the most important challenge to his personal diplomacy, as he tried to keep the Mexicans from going to the outer limit in their reaction to this incident.

Early in the ambassador's time there, in the spring of 1990, Vice President Dan Quayle visited Mexico City for a couple of days. On the last day the ambassador escorted him to a breakfast meeting with President Carlos Salinas. Quayle was scheduled to have a brief press conference after the breakfast and depart an hour and a half later for his next destination. They got through most of the breakfast, and Negroponte was relieved that the subject of the kidnapping hadn't come up.

With only a few minutes to go, however, Salinas suddenly said, "There's this small matter that I'd like to raise with you, Mr. Vice President." They then discussed the Alvarez Machain case for an hour, with Salinas concluding, "Well, because you've done that, I'm going to ask you to remove half of the DEA agents that you have in this country. And I want you to do it right away."

Somewhat to his own surprise, as this debate between the vice president and President Salinas continued, Negroponte found himself saying to both, "If you two keep this up much longer, you're going to precipitate a crisis in the United States-Mexico relationship." As a result both leaders backed down from their positions. President Salinas retracted his threat, or at least didn't press his request that we withdraw DEA personnel. Vice President Quayle was quite helpful in his press conference, and the issue sort of muddled along.

Then there arose new rules of the game—the United States was going to have to negotiate as to how the DEA would behave in Mexico. A couple of years later, the U.S. Supreme Court upheld our right to sequester and bring Alvarez Machain to trial, on the theory that there is no ground for questioning the way in which someone is brought before our courts, even if he is brought before the court from a foreign destination. At that the Mexicans reacted even more explosively than before.

Ambassador Negroponte was called in again, on the very night the Supreme Court decision was announced. He was confronted by the under secretary of the Mexican foreign ministry with a note stating that Mexico wished the United States to suspend its DEA program in its entirety. Taking a chapter out of previous service at another embassy, the ambassador simply returned the note directly to Under Secretary Andres

Rosenthal and said, "I don't know whether I'll do more harm to U.S.-Mexico relations by accepting this note or by returning it to you. So I think I'll just return it to you and not accept it." Fortunately that caused the Mexicans to think about the matter overnight, and once again, through a variety of diplomatic maneuverings, the embassy succeeded in pulling the host government back from a brinkmanship approach.

Swaziland

Mary Ryan served as the first woman ambassador of any country accredited to the southern African kingdom of Swaziland in its then-20 years as an independent state. U.S. foreign policy officialdom for a very long time subscribed to an unwritten and unproven theory that it was inappropriate and inadvisable to assign female ambassadors to most countries in the world, even after American presidents began naming a few women as chiefs of mission in the 1930s. It was widely believed that they could not function effectively in conservative Muslim countries, nor in the countries of Latin America, East Asia, and later Africa that were strongly patriarchal, where women were held in low estate and never played political roles. So our earliest women ambassadors were sent to European posts exclusively. But now, and in the past couple of decades, women have served ably in every conceivable country and society, even in some that remain staunchly male dominated in politics and government.

According to Ryan, "Women in Swaziland, despite the fact that they did most of the work in the country (as in most of the Third World), were valued significantly lower than the cattle Swazi men so prized." She was determined to change that and to raise Swazi consciousness on women's issues. So she accepted every invitation to speak that she received, in homesteads, parliament, grammar schools, high schools, and the university. Although she tried not to offend male sensibilities, she was relentless. Years later the Swazi high commissioner in Ottawa, a woman and the first to serve in such a post, said Ryan's example had encouraged her and other women to tell the men in charge in Swaziland that "the American ambassador is a woman and if she can do this and that, so can we."

When the Swazi government had received the request to approve Ryan's appointment as the new U.S. ambassador, it had decided, after considerable discussion, to treat her as an "honorary man," much as the whites ruling South Africa designated certain Asians as "honorary whites." She is glad that it was late in her tour before she learned this from a government minister, who informed her in greatest confidence and embarrassment. She believes that being a woman gained her access to certain places and people; because she was a curiosity, many Swazi officials confided things to her that they might not have told another man. She thinks she made a difference not only for Swaziland but also for the United States by being outspoken on women's issues in her country of assignment.

Australia

Australia has long been a close ally of the United States, among other things in five shooting wars. But there were major issues during Edward Perkins's tenure in Canberra: trade, nuclear concerns about the North Pacific, a chemical weapons ban treaty, a nuclear nonproliferation treaty, plus Australian unhappiness over agricultural subsidies for U.S. wheat producers to permit equal competition in markets where European farmers are aided by subsidies. Often believing that America takes their country for granted, the Australians were openly concerned about the relationship.

Determined to use public diplomacy to maximum effect, Perkins traveled widely, spoke at Rotary Club meetings and other social events, cultivated farmers' groups, met often with the cattlemen's association, visited high schools, grade schools, universities, and wineries, and met with environmental groups and the ecumenical community. He visited the constituencies of members of parliament representing farm communities, and almost every aboriginal community. Every Australian knew about the issues that had an impact on the U.S.-Australian relationship. These audiences were not always happy to hear the message, but they listened, commented, and perhaps in some cases changed their views. The point is that contact with a wide spectrum of the Australian populace to explain the views of the United States on questions of subsidies and trade was crucial. Perkins emphasizes that only an ambassador on the ground, traveling around the country and meeting with the people, can perform that task.

Assessing Ambassadorial Influence on Policy

Michael Armacost has offered a pointed assessment of ambassadorial policy influence. Based on his experiences at both ends of the policy seesaw—at major embassies abroad and on the seventh floor of the State Department, where the most senior American diplomats have their offices—he has some important caveats to offer his colleagues.

Although some cases cited herein represent the exceptional experiences of certain ambassadors, most ambassadors don't bring to their assignments the credentials that Robert Strauss, for example, brought from his background in domestic politics, and few are "policy entrepreneurs" of the caliber of Frank Carlucci, with his high-level experiences in the policy-making councils of the federal government. Most ambassadors, most of the time, execute rather than formulate policy. Most of the things they do in representation, negotiating, and reporting contribute only indirectly to the making of policy.

The analytic reasons for that division of labor are, first, that politicians and the aides who work closely with them tend to arrogate for themselves, quite properly, the right to define their objectives at home and abroad, and to seek and appropriate the monies needed to carry out those policies. That is Washington work, and ambassadors are not in Washington.

Second, the intensity of bureaucratic infighting in Washington is high, and the congressional weight in policy making is heavy, particularly in times of peace and prosperity. Therefore, ambassadors have difficulty timing their interventions in policy making in ways that take adequately into account the interplay among institutional interests and competing constituencies at home that have a major influence on policy.

If one asks, What are the conditions in which an ambassador can be effective, or what attributes of an ambassador enable him to play the policy game? the answer is that an ambassador has more of the perspective of a president than of a representative of a parochial agency because an ambassador has to oversee the activities of a whole host of agencies in his embassy. Consequently, the ambassador is a natural ally of those who are seeking to integrate policy in Washington, with a perspective that is quite different from that of many of the "advocacy" players back home.

Because the ambassador presides "where the rubber hits the road," and where many different policies are being implemented simultaneously, he often possesses a unique capacity to spot where a policy has run out of gas, no longer responds to the existing circumstances; and he can often spot emerging problems on the ground for which no effective policy has been formulated. As Washington veterans know, moreover, "he who initiates the draft governs," that is, those who get in early and shape the definition of the problem have a capacity to influence the outcome. Ambassadors often find themselves in that situation.

Most important, says Armacost—and the accounts in this book provide illustrations of the point—more and more of the objectives of the United States involve changing the contours of politics and economics in other countries. Uncertainty about an important political evolution abroad maximizes the role of an ambassador in policy making, especially if the country is important to the United States and if local conditions are in flux and thus open to change.

A Contrarian View

Former Ambassador and Assistant Secretary of State Arthur Hummel* is impressed by the changes that have affected our diplomacy during the 30 years since his first ambassadorship. He sees a marked drift toward Washington and away from the slice of policy making that ambassadors and embassies used to have, a trend he believes is unlikely to change.

In support of this view, he cites four reasons: The digital mode of transmission of telegrams has meant much faster communication between Washington and its embassies abroad. In addition, very few posts had secure telephones decades ago. Secure telephones are a dangerous instrument in that ambassadors can now receive oral instructions from high officials in Washington, including from agencies other than the State Department, without the benefit of a paper record.

Second is congressional micromanagement, which has increased over the years. Third is Washington's control over resources, especially the funds managed by the other agencies that now have representatives serving abroad, along with their larger share in the policy making that goes on in Washington. Last is media reporting—not just by CNN but by the print media as well—and its influence on policy making, all of which, Hummel believes, has diminished the input provided by ambassadors.

Changing the President's Mind

On the question of when and how diplomats influence or shape foreign policy, former Ambassador and Foreign Service Institute Director Stephen Low** cites three instances in which foreign policy considerations eventually prevailed over the known and publicly stated views of the president as seen from the Washington perspective: the Panama Canal negotiations, the Philippine crisis, and South African sanctions.

Three successive American presidents expressed support for keeping U.S. control of the Panama Canal but were persuaded to negotiate its reversion to the Panamanians. By about 1970, when the U.S. Navy recognized that a two-ocean Navy did not require the canal and that it could

---

* He served as ambassador to Burma, Ethiopia, Pakistan, and China and in Washington as assistant secretary of state for East Asian and Pacific affairs.

** His posts as ambassador were Zambia and Nigeria.

be more of a liability than an asset, the Defense Department had come around to the State Department's point of view that we needed to negotiate a reversion agreement. When Low was serving as the staff member for Latin America on the National Security Council, he had sent to his boss, Kissinger, then the national security adviser, a set of negotiating instructions on the canal, carefully worked out between State and Defense. The two men were on a plane flying back to Washington from a meeting of the Organization of American States in Santiago, Chile. Kissinger was using the flight to catch up on paperwork when he came upon Low's memo. He strode back to the rear of the plane where the NSC staffers were seated, threw the memo he had just approved with his signature into Low's lap, and said: "Nixon hates this . . . but he will sign."

In the case of the Philippines, President Reagan personally liked President Marcos and supported him fully. Consistent with Armacost's perspective from Manila cited earlier in this chapter, Low recalls that it took a lot of persuasion to get the reluctant president to change his attitude and therefore our policy toward Marcos. Among those in Washington who were influential were Paul Wolfowitz at State, Richard Armitage at Defense, and Gaston Sigur, the NSC staff member for East Asia at the White House. But a crucial briefing of the president also came from Admiral Crowe, then our senior military commander for the Pacific based in Hawaii.

South Africa was a quite different case. The United States had no troops stationed there. But President Reagan had gone on record defending the South African government despite its apartheid policies and practices. In that situation it required Congress, reacting to an effective lobbying campaign organized by black activist Randall Robinson, to rally to the position advocated by the State Department and to force adoption of a different policy—a stronger sanctions regime—over the president's opposition.

Ambassador Low draws four lessons from these cases. (1) If you wish to shape or change a policy you must have powerful allies elsewhere in the executive branch and/or in Congress. (2) Purely foreign policy views can prevail, changing the position of a president, in cases that are not central to U.S. national security. (3) Where U.S. troops or bases are involved, the Defense Department's support is indispensable. (4) When State, Defense, and the White House national security staff are all in agreement, they can pursue policy changes effectively even when the president is not initially inclined in the same direction.

Managing Crisis Situations

One of the worst terrorist incidents affecting the American diplomatic service occurred in Khartoum, Sudan, in early March 1973. It was a hostage-taking operation by the Palestinian group "Black September," which had taken that name after the confrontation between Palestinian guerrillas and the Jordanian army in Jordan in the fall of 1970. The previous September that group had been responsible for the massacre of 11 Israeli athletes at the Munich Olympic Games, a terrorist action directed at Israel, which had been pressured, unsuccessfully, to release some 200 Palestinian prisoners. In 1973 the terrorists' ultimate target was the Jordanian government. A small team of well-armed commandos invaded the residence of the Saudi Arabian ambassador to Sudan, who was hosting a farewell party for the departing American chargé d'affaires ad interim, George Curtis Moore, who had just been replaced by the newly accredited American ambassador, Cleo A. Noel Jr. The two American diplomats and the Belgian chargé, Guy Eid, were bound and taken to the basement and held there as hostages. The commandos demanded the release of some of their colleagues imprisoned in Jordan, especially Abu Daud, one of their leaders, and threatened to kill the hostages if their demands were not met.

President Nixon dispatched the State Department's under secretary for management, William Macomber, to Khartoum as his special representative to deal with the situation, but also made a public announcement that the U.S. government does not negotiate with terrorists. Macomber's arrival was delayed by a dust storm over Egypt, and while he was still in the air the commandos, having heard the statement that there would be no negotiations, proceeded to murder the three hostages in cold blood.

The no-negotiations policy, and the refusal to release prisoners, pay ransom, or meet other demands of terrorists, are sound principles in the abstract, but the fact is that lives are sometimes saved in such situations by a willingness at least to talk. The dispatch of a special representative from Washington was probably a good idea in this case, as a tactic to gain time, and was necessitated by the fact that the American officials on the ground who would normally deal with a terrorist incident were the very victims being held as hostages, the No. 1 and No. 2 officers of the American Embassy.*

In other cases our diplomats have dealt heroically and effectively with crises of this kind. Robert Dillon was our ambassador in Lebanon in April 1983 when the embassy was almost completely destroyed by a massive car bomb, causing the loss of many Lebanese and American lives. The attack was so sudden and unexpected that the role of the ambassador, who escaped with minor injuries, became dealing with the aftermath, not the incident itself.

Dealing With a Hostage Crisis

In an earlier assignment, as deputy chief of mission in Kuala Lumpur, Malaysia, Dillon coped with one of the most difficult hostage-taking incidents experienced by an American diplomatic mission. On a steaming hot morning in August 1975, Dillon was seated at his desk on the 12th floor of the American International Assurance (AIA) building in downtown Kuala Lumpur. The offices of the American Embassy occupied the building's top 2½ floors. Ambassador Frank Underhill was in the United States on home leave, leaving Dillon in charge. Most of the embassy's staff occupied the top two floors, but the consular section filled half of the 10th floor, the other half housing the Swedish Embassy. An American Marine guard controlled access to the 11th and 12th floors, but not to the 10th, which was open to the public. The building had four elevators: three for passengers opened into a lobby on each floor, and a fourth, for freight, opened in the opposite direction into a stairwell.

Suddenly Dillon heard small-arms fire. A staff member rushed in to say the shooting was on the 10th floor. Dillon, the sergeant in charge of the Marine guard detachment, and the embassy security officer picked up weapons and made their way down the stairs. The three passenger elevators were jammed open on the 10th floor. The freight elevator, however, was working. In the stairwell were a wounded Malaysian security guard and a Marine, both of whom had exchanged fire with unseen adversaries. The wounded Malaysian was evacuated via the freight elevator and taken to a hospital.

Several Malaysian policemen arrived on the ninth floor and sealed off the 10th floor. Unknown gunmen were holding the 10th floor, the passenger elevators were out of commission, and the stairwell was unusable

---

* David Korn gives a full account of this episode in his book *Assassination in Khartoum*, Indiana University Press, 1993.

because it would expose anyone using it to the gunmen. The slow and unreliable freight elevator was the only means of reaching the outside world. Dillon and his colleagues did not know how many gunmen were involved, who they were, and what they wanted.

Although the air conditioning had stopped working, making the offices unbearably hot, the telephones were working. Dillon phoned the State Department's operations center to report the little he knew at that stage and then took the freight elevator down to meet with senior Malaysian security officials who had arrived to take charge on the ground floor. The deputy prime minister (later prime minister), Hussein Onn, arrived and immediately named Ghazali Shafei, the interior minister, as the official in charge. Offers of assistance arrived by telephone from the diplomatic missions of Britain, Canada, Australia, and New Zealand, and alternate communications facilities were established in the Canadian Embassy. In exchanges of fire with a terrorist shooting from a 10th-floor window, a Malaysian security officer was seriously wounded, and two policemen were lightly wounded. There were no further casualties during the incident, which lasted 4½ days.

Five hours into the standoff the embassy's Malaysian telephone operator said to Dillon: "The terrorist leader wants to speak to you." Dillon started to take the phone but then remembered having read that the chief decision maker should always stay one step removed in a negotiating situation. So he told his economic officer, Richard Jackson, to take the phone, and for the next 4½ days the latter's carefully modulated, unthreatening baritone was the embassy's link with the terrorists.

At about the same time, the terrorists threw a note out a window, perversely shooting and wounding the policeman who ran to pick it up. Between the note and Jackson's conversation with the tense and erratic terrorist leader, the Americans learned that the consular section on the 10th floor had been seized by a group of Japanese Red Army (JRA) terrorists and that they were holding many hostages, including the head of the section, Robert Stebbins. The terrorists issued a series of demands to the Japanese government, whose deputy foreign minister had just arrived in Washington, an event that accounted for the timing of the attack. The JRA men threatened to start shooting their hostages if their demands were not met.

The Swedish chargé and his secretary were hiding in their offices while maintaining telephone contact with Stockholm. It was 24 hours before the JRA men discovered they had additional, potentially valuable hostages. The Malaysians established a command center on the first floor chaired by Shafei and staffed by the Japanese ambassador, two senior Malaysian police officials, and Dillon. The American mission's public affairs officer, Haynes Mahoney, set up a press center several blocks away, handling the dozens of correspondents who poured into Kuala Lumpur, as well as taking hundreds of phone calls from news organizations, TV and radio stations, and family members of hostages. He correctly guided the reporters to understand that this was first of all a Malaysian show.

The AIA building was now isolated by a monumental traffic jam. Phone calls poured in from the State Department. Al LaPorta, acting chief of the political section, manned the phone, instructed by Dillon to say the chargé was out and to please leave a message for him. At one point LaPorta said exactly that to Secretary Kissinger, who was telephoning from his airplane at the Belgrade airport to check on the situation. In fact Dillon hardly slept at all during those 4½ days, which he says was a mistake, because he became terribly tired and should have taken care to maintain his health and alertness.

On the fifth day of the crisis a peaceful resolution was achieved when the Japanese government released four JRA prisoners and flew them to Kuala Lumpur. A fifth JRA prisoner refused to be released, causing a crisis within a crisis until a telephone call was patched through from his Kyoto prison and he persuaded the terrorist leader that he really did want to stay in prison. An exchange of prisoners for hostages was arranged at the airport, where it was established for the first time that there were five terrorists.

The prisoner-hostage exchange was an excruciating experience and took several hours. The terrorists and their 50 hostages were driven to the airport in blacked-out buses, and the exchange proceeded with about 12 hostages traded for each released JRA prisoner. As part of the agreement the JRA removed the explosives they had installed in the walls of the consular section. The Americans knew about these explosives, as CIA technicians had dropped microphones down through the walls and had picked up snatches of the terrorists' conversations. The explosives were blown up at the airport before the Japanese plane took off. The huge explosion and resulting crater gave Dillon some pause. He had been aware that he and his colleagues had been sitting atop explosives for more than four days, but he had not grasped how powerful they were.

The JRA group flew off to Libya. The final steps toward ending the crisis included persuading the Libyans to receive the plane and obtaining the agreement of a very reluctant Sri Lankan government to permit the plane to refuel on that island. The terrorists were accompanied on the flight by the four released prisoners and four new hostages—two Japanese and two Malaysian—who had been volunteered by their governments to replace the original 50 American, Swedish, Malaysian, and Australian hostages. All four men eventually returned safely to Malaysia. One of the courageous Japanese, Kyohei Murata, later became his country's ambassador in Washington. He and the other able Japanese negotiators received no thanks from the Malaysian government, which complained that they had dragged their feet in the negotiations. For example, Shafei, the interior minister, said to them, referring to World War II: "You overran our whole goddamned country in less time than you're taking to deal with this situation."

The thanks offered to the Japanese by the American side consisted of several lectures delivered by Dillon on instructions from the secretary of state about the inadvisability of negotiating with terrorists. Not surprisingly, the Japanese found the admonitions from Washington gratuitous. The last hostage released at the airport was the American consul, Stebbins, whose poise and example as the leader of the hostages preserved their morale throughout the ordeal. Had the JRA carried out its threat to start executing hostages, Stebbins would have been the first victim.

Ambassador Dillon's experience in Malaysia better equipped him to deal with other crises that arose when he served in Turkey and Lebanon and particularly when he was deputy commissioner general of UNRWA, the large United Nations organization for the Palestinian refugees in the Near East. The first lesson learned from the episode in Kuala Lumpur, he says, was the need to reduce the vulnerability to terrorist invasion of our embassy premises in capitals throughout the world. Another lesson well understood by diplomats serving abroad, but less well at the upper levels of the U.S. government in Washington, is that the person managing the crisis on the spot does not control the environment. He may be the person in charge of the American side of the operation, but he can't just order people around, as much as Washington would like him to. Every action and every decision must be negotiated with the other governments involved, including a host government that may have an agenda quite different from our own.

Dillon stresses that the negotiating skills and cultural sensitivity developed over many years of service by career diplomats become crucial in managing a crisis on someone else's turf. Another important asset is the teamwork developed over time by the key officers of an embassy, so that they can work together harmoniously and use their established good relationships with host government officials to find solutions with minimal conflict. In a crisis there is no substitute for having on your team experienced people who know and trust one another. According to Dillon, the bottom line on crisis management is that it has to be done locally, not directed from Washington.

Dealing With Internal Chaos: Philippines and Egypt

Philippines

The period from August 1987 to July 1991, when Nicholas Platt was U.S. ambassador to the Philippines,* was a time of great political and military turbulence in that country and of suffering caused by natural disasters. Major crises with which our embassy in Manila had to cope included two violent coup attempts against the Aquino government, the assassination and murder of 10 American citizens, the kidnapping of a Peace Corps volunteer by Communist rebels and the subsequent evacuation of the Peace Corps, a killer earthquake, four supertyphoons, and the eruption of Mount Pinatubo, which destroyed Clark Air Force Base and required the relocation of 29,000 American service personnel.

Of these crises, the most complex and dangerous from the embassy's point of view was the second coup attempt by army rebels to overthrow Corazon Aquino's government. The attempt began on November 29, 1989, and lasted more than a week. There were three phases: first, a day of dramatic air attacks on Malacanang Palace, which required U.S. intervention in the form of "demonstration flights" by F-4's stationed at Clark; second, a two-day ground battle over control of army headquarters in Manila; and finally, a six-day war of nerves over the fate of several hundred Americans and other foreign nationals trapped in the hotels of the Makati business district, which was occupied by frustrated rebel soldiers.

The embassy survived this series of events without loss of life and with a great deal of help from the U.S. Navy's Seals and the U.S. Marines. Ambassador Platt says the embassy's experience demonstrated the crucial importance of information handling in embassy crisis management. The quality and the credibility of the information that the ambassador passes on to his staff and to the American community during a crisis will determine the degree of their responsiveness in a time of maximum dan-

---

* He also served as ambassador to Zambia and as executive secretary of the Department of State.

ger. If the ambassador levels with them throughout the crisis, contrary to a natural instinct not to upset people by telling them how serious the ambassador thinks the situation actually is, they will do as they are asked and follow instructions from the embassy. It is important to avoid passing on unsubstantiated intelligence and to filter out clearly spurious rumors. That is what provides the credibility needed to obtain everyone's cooperation.

Platt illustrates this point with the following account. The embassy learned at 2 a.m. on December 5, the sixth day of the coup crisis, that the government was planning to drive the rebels out of the Makati business district by force. Its idea was to bombard Makati and drive the rebels into the Forbes Park area, a neighborhood where 3,000 Americans lived. The embassy asked the government to give it two hours at least before launching the attack. The ambassador made this appeal personally to Aquino, and she agreed. The embassy then used its extensive radio network, which had been carefully prepared over many months, to alert the community, and in the next 90 minutes 3,000 people were evacuated from the area into safer parts of the city. And, Platt adds, "They didn't ask any questions, except perhaps 'Can we bring the dog?' to which the answer was 'No.' If you level with your people, they will do as you say when you most want them to."

Egypt

The leadership of an ambassador can be absolutely essential to maintaining the morale of the official and private American community during a troubled time, not only for their sake but to maintain good relations with the host government and its people. Frank Wisner recalls such an occasion when he was serving as ambassador in Egypt. His decisions and actions did not result from instructions received from Washington but were instinctive and grew out of his deep understanding of what needed to be done to maintain our good relations with Egypt.

It was during the Persian Gulf War in 1991. Saddam Hussein's aggression began as a threat to the neighboring countries from his land forces. But very quickly that threat became a missile threat. And it then became a "street" threat in the sense that sympathizers with his particular brand of Arab radicalism could endanger the lives of American citizens and the survival of American embassies. Throughout the region affected by the war, in official and unofficial American communities, wives and children were evacuated. Often American corporations made decisions to take families, or employees and their families, out of the Middle East. This created a huge problem, for it was a time when the U.S. presence was critical. We were at the core of the coalition against Saddam. Embassy officers and American businessmen played important roles in maintaining relationships during the course of the Gulf conflict.

Wisner was presented with a dilemma. The Cairo embassy was very large, with more than 1,000 staff members. He had no direct instructions on how to deal with the threat to his community. The only instruction was: "When you deem the situation unsafe for your people to continue to be there and it's unsafe for your American community, you should take whatever actions are necessary and recommend evacuation." He made the decision on his own that it would be wise to try to keep an American presence in Egypt, and he devised his own strategies to accomplish that.

He worked very closely with the American school, for if the school closed its doors, lots of people would go home. He organized weekly town meetings to which literally hundreds and hundreds of people would come and ask their most pressing and anxious questions. He personally corresponded with a variety of corporations, trying to discourage them from pulling out their people even though he knew they faced legal liabilities if harm befell any of their employees. He took these measures because in his judgment the security situation was adequate to protect Americans.

His actions sent a strong signal to the Egyptians that we stood with them. They were grateful that the Americans had sufficient confidence in them that the embassy would trust keeping U.S. citizens in their land. The Gulf War was a time of extreme national importance in Egypt, and American corporations played a vital supportive role. The French, Germans, and other nationalities left the area, making the Americans stand out as people who had stood by their Egyptian friends, something that will long be remembered.

Ambassador Wisner ran a decided risk with the course he took, not least to his own reputation and judgment. He was not pressured by Washington to order an evacuation, but he was asked to keep the situation under very careful review. He was frequently asked to provide his current assessment, and Washington accepted his judgment as the ambassador.

Some American corporations cooperated with his effort to maintain an American presence; others did not. Wisner judges his effort was successful with about 75 percent of the American corporate community. The situation was especially tense on the day that Delta Airlines ceased flying. How was the embassy going to get people home if they had to be evacuated? Most airlines had stopped serving the Middle East. The tension eventually abated, and normalcy returned. Wisner stresses that people long remember how other people behave during troubled times.

Dealing With Political and Military Violence: Liberia and Somalia

Liberia

James Bishop faced one crisis after another as ambassador in Liberia and Somalia.* Each country came apart in slow motion during his watch, creating recurrent crises affecting substantial U.S. interests. These could only be managed locally, he insists, not by e-mail or by fax from Washington. Success depended on the bonds of trust that had been created with local officials and on face-to-face discussions with heads of state. When the Department of State did try to implement policy from Washington, U.S. interests suffered.

"If you can keep your people quiet, I'll get your guys back for you," promised the commanding general of the Armed Forces of Liberia (AFL) when Bishop asked for his help in saving the lives of two Americans arrested for participation in the latest unsuccessful antigovernment coup plot. The Liberian plotters were all dead, summarily executed when discovered moving under arms from the border toward the capital. The two Americans were to be tried for treason, a capital offense.

"It's the frizzy-haired American ambassador," the public address system boomed as Bishop, accompanied by his wife, arrived for his first encounter with the AFL to attend a parade inside the Monrovia garrison. Similar familiarity marked many subsequent contacts, reflecting both the sloppiness of the AFL and the intimacy of U.S.-Liberian relations. General Henry Dubar, the AFL commander, was more reserved when they first met. But after taking each other's measure over drinks at the home of the U.S. military mission chief, they each decided they could deal with the other frankly.

Dubar had satisfied Bishop that he could deliver earlier in the year, after President Samuel K. Doe and Bishop had had the first of their semi-public spats. Learning one afternoon that Doe planned to arrest the most prominent opposition politician the next day, Bishop had sent Doe a personal letter warning him that he would harm bilateral relations if he were to make that move. Shortly thereafter the ambassador raised a ruckus

---

* He also served as ambassador to Niger.

when two of the embassy's drivers were beaten up by Doe's security people merely because they had overtaken Doe while he was driving through the capital late at night in an unmarked car. After Doe refused to speak to Bishop for several months, Dubar had sought the ambassador out, together with the minister of defense and the head of the national security service. The three officials volunteered to try to reconcile Doe and the ambassador. Bishop agreed, and they persuaded Doe to resume normal contacts.

Now, the lives of two Americans were at stake. The embassy made the usual consular representations, obtained access to the prisoners, and provided food and other material assistance. But despite congressional threats of sanctions, public complaints from family members, and criticism in the American press, embassy and State Department rhetoric was deliberately kept muted. A persuasive deputy chief of mission and a credible consular officer even talked Ramsey Clark into holding his fire when the former attorney general came to Monrovia to seek the release of the two would-be coup makers. Shortly thereafter, four months after their arrest, the two Americans were on their way home.

The next crisis involved a U.S. initiative to end an aid program. "We'll bring this to an end without blaming anyone," Bishop told Foreign Minister Rudolph Johnson when first informing him that the United States was withdrawing its financial experts from Liberia. Sent to the country 11 months earlier on the personal instructions of Secretary Shultz and USAID Administrator Peter McPherson, their mission had been a last-ditch attempt to check government corruption and preserve international assistance. The controls they had established were being so massively evaded by Liberian officials and complicit foreign bankers that Bishop had decided no further expenditure of U.S. government funds could be justified on a project that had already cost American taxpayers $10 million.

The embassy by this time was no stranger to confrontation with Doe and his government. Bishop had used the press repeatedly to correct government disinformation. His meetings with Doe and his ministers had become increasingly heated as evidence of their subversion of the control regime accumulated. Both the Liberian and the American public would ultimately learn the details of what had gone wrong. But the ambassador's immediate priority was seeing that the 17 experts and their families were able to leave Liberia without harassment or injury. They had no diplomatic status and thus were quite vulnerable to government retaliation. One expert had already been threatened by a Doe insider who had pointed a pistol at him. Doe's entourage included psychopaths capable of murder, and his minister of information delighted in trying to stir up anti-American sentiment.

Foreign Minister Johnson and Ambassador Bishop had previously had many policy differences to discuss. But Johnson's service in a corrupt regime had not eroded all moral principle. An intelligent man with considerable diplomatic experience, he also could be expected to recognize the benefits to his government of bringing the experts' mission to a conclusion as a no-fault divorce. The State Department was even more concerned than Bishop that Doe would respond hostilely to the news that the United States was unilaterally terminating the mission. It therefore proved an easy task to obtain a letter to Doe from President Reagan. Avoiding a New York Times correspondent who had arrived in Monrovia to write about the situation, Bishop flew to Doe's hometown to deliver President Reagan's letter. Doe was so flattered by the presidential attention, and so mollified by the foreign minister's news of the no-fault formulation, that the experts were able to depart Liberia without incident.

Subsequent open warfare in Liberia highlighted the value of the official American presence. The American government had too many important interests to protect to countenance closing down the embassy and evacuating its diplomats when danger threatened. In Liberia there were irreplaceable Voice of America and CIA facilities, and unrestricted access to Robertsfield Airport, through which we were provisioning guerrillas contesting the Soviet and Cuban military presence in Angola. Liberia was also host to 5,000 American citizens, many so closely integrated into Liberian society that they would be very reluctant to evacuate.

"Stall," Ambassador Bishop cabled Washington when Doe asked him for U.S. military aid under the terms of our bilateral defense accord days after Charles Taylor invaded the country. The embassy needed time both to gauge the seriousness of the latest coup attempt and to see how the notoriously incompetent and brutal AFL would respond. The answers were not long in coming. The coup was not going to be another flash in the pan, and the AFL's violence against civilians was driving recruits into the rebel ranks. Meanwhile, the government would not even acknowledge that its citizens were being internally displaced, let alone try to assist them. Monrovia was awash in misinformation and disinformation, and American citizens naturally were confused.

Doe was not pleased when Bishop told him there would be no U.S. military aid for his forces and urged him to assign more competent commanders. When Washington broadcast the press guidance the embassy had prepared condemning the human rights violations of both belligerent parties, Doe's ire increased. When Bishop pressed him to extend a hand of friendship to the tribes the AFL had abused, and to initiate relief programs for the internally displaced persons (IDPs), he stonewalled.

It had been U.S. policy to keep sufficient distance from Doe to be able to work with a successor regime. The embassy's access to the government allowed it to track its performance closely. When Doe finally agreed to replace his military commander in the field, Bishop sent the American military mission chief to the combat zone to observe the AFL's performance under the new leadership. Within 10 days the chief reported that the AFL remained incompetent and abusive. When it became clear that the government would not request assistance for helping its IDPs, the ambassador declared a disaster unilaterally and gave $25,000 to the International Committee of the Red Cross to help truck in food to the displaced. The government's consequent criticism suited the American objective of putting greater distance between the United States and the Liberian regime. Meanwhile, the embassy's access provided good information to use in briefing American citizens and allied members of the diplomatic corps.

Based on the American military mission chief's field reports, and on Doe's decision to expand the AFL by recruiting hoodlums off the streets, Bishop recommended to Washington that he be authorized to tell Doe that we would announce publicly the suspension of our bilateral military assistance relationship. It was at that point that the State Department decided to become involved in the tactics of our diplomacy. But bureaucratic difficulties in deciding on tactics in an interagency setting compounded by unfamiliarity with the details of the Monrovia environment produced gridlock and missed opportunity.

The State Department decided that the message to Doe should come from the president and be delivered by a high-level special envoy. But the White House had no appetite for a scenario that would involve President Bush in the mess in Monrovia. As more weeks went by, an effort was made to engage Secretary Baker, with identical results. Finally, despite the embassy's warning that Doe would refuse to receive him, a deputy assistant secretary was sent to Monrovia with a letter. By the time he arrived, and was received at the foreign ministry rather than at the executive mansion, the rebels were moving on Monrovia. The opportunity to distance ourselves further from the depredations of Doe's soldiers was gone. We could not further endanger the 5,000 American citizens, who soon would require evacuation, by antagonizing the Liberian soldiers through whose checkpoints the evacuees would have to pass. Bishop had done all he could.

Somalia

At the end of his tour in Liberia, Bishop was named ambassador to Somalia, which had been without a U.S. ambassador for nearly a year. It was an "out of the frying pan and into the fire" experience, but Bishop's arrival in Mogadishu was delayed for five months while he headed a task force in Washington dealing with the rapidly deteriorating situation in Liberia. When he finally did arrive in Somalia, the conditions were depressingly familiar. Three rebel armies were challenging the regime in the field, and terrorism and banditry were daily fare in the capital. The buildup to the Gulf War (code-named "Desert Shield") was in its second month, as hundreds of thousands of American service personnel headed toward the Persian Gulf.

Our policy at the time was to urge the Somali government to negotiate with its domestic opponents and critics, and to insist that the government do more to protect the local American community—one Marine had already been shot. At the same time, we were trying to preserve our military access rights. Implementing these policies required close attention to the dynamics of the regime and to the moods of the Somali president.

In a one-on-one meeting with President Siad Barre at the end of 1990, Bishop inquired about his game plan for confronting the mounting violence in and around Mogadishu. When the president replied that the fate of his government depended upon God's will, it was evident he was slipping. The embassy had already evacuated dependents and nonessential personnel. It prepared to reduce its ranks further, strengthen its physical defenses, and refine its contingency planning. But before anyone else could depart, the city exploded with such violence that it became too dangerous for Americans to leave the embassy compound.

While gunfire and the occasional rocket flew over and sometimes landed inside the walls of the compound, the 37 official Americans who remained, along with loyal Somali employees who shared their risks, provided shelter, food, and medicine to the more than 200 private Americans and expatriates, as well as many family members of the Somali staff, who were in their care. The evacuees helicoptered to the carrier Guam when it finally arrived, among them nationals of other foreign governments, were quite pleased with the protection afforded them by the U.S. Foreign Service. Most of the governments whose diplomats (including 10 chiefs of mission) and civilians disembarked five days later in Oman were effusive in expressing their appreciation. Secretary Baker apparently scored a few points with his Soviet counterpart when the latter learned that we had arranged to have all Soviet diplomatic staff escorted from their ransacked embassy to the American compound in time to board the Marine helicopters.

As with Liberia, we had good reasons not to close our embassy in Somalia and evacuate our diplomats. In Somalia we had military access rights and pre-positioned fuel supplies to enable U.S. military forces to respond to precisely the type of threat to Middle East oil fields that Saddam Hussein initiated in 1990. U.S. military access to Somalia's ports and airfields ultimately proved unnecessary because the Saudis permitted coalition forces to deploy on their territory. But maintaining our diplomatic presence for as long as possible in Somalia not only helped save a substantial number of American and allied lives but also permitted the United States to keep sufficient pressure on the regime to forestall any sellout to the Iraqis before the Somali government ceased to function in the American diplomats' final days at the compound. The U.S. Marines and Navy Seals who put their lives at grave risk by flying 450 miles over the open sea at night to land in a compound that the American diplomats had already been forced to use gunfire to protect were delighted to put their training to what they considered a worthwhile use.

Somalia Revisited

After the evacuation of our embassy in Mogadishu, the country fell into general anarchy, with a civil war among competing, violent clans and tremendous suffering by the population. By late November 1992 some 300,000 Somalis had died of starvation and disease, and as many more were seriously threatened with death over the next six months. Ships carrying food for relief were being shelled and could not make port. Food in the port could not get through to the starving because of warlords, militias, and bandits. A 500-man UN peacekeeping force was pinned down in Mogadishu and rendered ineffectual. Food delivered by the U.S. Air Force and other relief flights to the interior had little effect because of militia and bandit interference.

On November 25, 1992, President Bush, nearing the end of his term in office, decided that the United States would undertake a humanitarian relief effort, led by elements of one Marine and one Army division, with broad international participation and the approval of the UN Security Council. The operation received the Pentagon code name

"Operation Restore Hope" and the Security Council acronym UNITAF (Unified International Task Force). The mission was "to establish a secure environment for relief operations" in that part of Somalia most affected by the famine and civil war, to be followed by a UN peacekeeping force. The Bush administration had no long-term plan for the political or economic rehabilitation of Somalia. As a lame-duck president, Bush understandably chose to leave long-term issues to the United Nations and to President-elect Clinton.

During the White House meeting at which President Bush approved the plan presented by the secretaries of defense and state, Robert Oakley's name was proposed and approved for assignment to Somalia to provide high-level, experienced diplomatic input for UNITAF and to help coordinate civilian activities of the United States, other governments, UN agencies, and non-governmental organizations. Oakley had the requisite background for this task, as he had served as the U.S. ambassador to Somalia a decade earlier. He had retired from the Foreign Service, but on receiving a call from General Colin Powell that he was needed in Somalia, he had only one answer. There was almost no time for preparation in Washington, either by the military or by Oakley, as the initial landing in Somalia took place 12 days after the presidential decision.

A detailed account of this combination diplomatic-military relief operation, which lasted about three months, is beyond the scope of this book,* but it does illustrate how our senior diplomats these days are often deployed in unusual projects with unique responsibilities, not just as ambassadors heading embassies. Several things are worth noting that help explain why this operation was successful. To begin, Oakley was able to obtain a superb staff, including three political officers who had served in Somalia in the previous two years, a USAID-provided disaster assistance response team of young men and women who knew the country well after having already served there for six months to a year, and a deputy, John Hirsch, who a decade earlier had been Ambassador Oakley's deputy chief of mission in Mogadishu.

Civilian-military teamwork was essential. Although Oakley had not met the senior American military officers before, they had shared prior experiences that prepared them well for the tasks in Somalia. The UNITAF commander, Lt. General Robert Johnston, and Oakley had both

---

* Ambassador Oakley's service in this special assignment to Somalia is covered in the book he wrote with John L. Hirsch entitled *Somalia and Operation Restore Hope: Reflections on Peacemaking and Peacekeeping*, U.S. Institute of Peace, 1995.

served in Lebanon (the general had put Yasir Arafat on the ship when the Palestine Liberation Organization was evacuated from Beirut), and Johnston had been chief of staff for Operation Desert Storm in the Gulf War. Maj. General Charles Wilhelm, Brig. General Anthony Zinni, and Oakley had all served in Vietnam, and Zinni had been chief of staff for Operation Provide Comfort in northern Iraq. These military officers were keenly aware of the political sensitivities involved in their work. Oakley also obtained the services of a number of former Somali employees of the closed Mogadishu embassy, who provided invaluable local knowledge and contacts.

With their previous experiences still vividly in mind, Oakley and the military officers knew the traps that were present; they wished to avoid the outcomes in Vietnam, where America had gotten itself in a quagmire, and in Beirut, where we had unconsciously become a party to other people's civil war, ending with the bombing of our embassy and Marine barracks. Even before the military landed in Mogadishu, Oakley contacted the two principal faction leaders in the capital area, Mohamed Ali Madhi and Mohammed Farah Aideed, and explained to them that the United States was coming to provide temporary humanitarian help, not to occupy the country or dictate to the Somalis, and that we did not want any fighting. Moreover, this was essentially the same force that had so easily defeated the Iraqi army in 1991, and therefore it would be unwise and dangerously futile to resist it. The clan leaders agreed, and the landing was unopposed.

The United States commanded tremendous firepower but used it with a remarkable degree of restraint given the chaotic conditions in Somalia. Inevitably there was some fighting, and Oakley developed an interesting tactic for dealing with these incidents. Each time there was a firefight with a particular group, Oakley, accompanied by one of the American generals, would sit down afterward with the faction's leader to deliver this message: "We assume that you didn't wish to declare war on us, so this must have been an accident, right?" The leader would agree that, yes, it had been an accident. Oakley would then say: "OK, use your radio to tell your people it was an accident, you're not at war with the United States, and it won't happen again." This technique helped prevent the development of basic enmity between the Somali factions and the U.S. forces.

A major achievement was the establishment of a humanitarian operations center to coordinate the work of all of the foreign relief groups in the country. The statistics are impressive. In six months it supervised the activities of some 60 relief organizations and supported over 235 security convoys, 130 unprotected relief convoys, and the delivery of about 40,000 tons of grain and the equivalent of 200 million meals. UNITAF also constructed or repaired some 2,300 kilometers of roads and nine airfields for both military and relief use.

The Bush administration, with total support from Oakley, General Johnston, and other force contributors, rejected UN Secretary General Boutros Boutros-Ghali's insistence that UNITAF disarm, forcibly if necessary, the many Somali factions and bandits, which would have brought on innumerable firefights. In early January 1993 the Somali faction leaders agreed in principle to voluntary disarmament, and an implementation plan was worked out. However, disagreement between UNITAF and UN headquarters over how to implement the disarmament resulted in its not being attempted by the time the UN peacekeeping force replaced UNITAF in May 1993. The UN force's mandate included forcible disarmament, but it was a weaker force and had no understanding with the Somalis on this issue. The opportunity for voluntary disarmament had been lost, and weapons of all kinds have since proliferated unchecked throughout Somalia.

In March Oakley returned to civilian life in Washington. Although an American, Admiral Jonathan Howe, became the UN secretary general's special representative in Somalia, the United States moved back to a supporting political and military role, and the Washington interagency task force backing Oakley's mission in Somalia was disbanded. The bloody battle in Mogadishu on October 3-4, 1993, a tragedy that resulted in so many U.S. soldiers being killed and wounded, led to a decision to withdraw U.S. forces. The following day Oakley was asked to return to Somalia as President Clinton's special representative. But, he says, "that is another story."

Diplomatic Crisis Management: Japan

The nature of diplomatic crisis management is that it is almost impossible to predict the character of the next crisis to be faced, when it will happen, or how it can best be managed. Improvisation is the name of the game. And that is why a crisis must be managed almost entirely locally, by the embassy in the field. Japan is one country where one would not expect to have to deal with many crises. This was not the case during Walter Mondale's tenure as ambassador.

First came the devastating Kobe earthquake. Many Americans were living there, the Osaka consulate's staff housing was where the earthquake hit, and the American consul general and his wife nearly lost their lives. The earthquake produced numerous casualties, a terrified populace, and major economic damage.

The Tokyo embassy's quick response was crucial, both to help its own traumatized personnel and to be as helpful as possible to the Japanese. The embassy immediately organized a task force. People were sent to Osaka to go door to door, looking for Americans. The U.S. military forces offered help, some members volunteering on their own, but that could only be given in response to a request by the host authorities. The embassy also offered to send health specialists, medicines, and other kinds of assistance. The foreign minister of Japan later presented a citation to the commander of the American forces, at a ceremony in which Ambassador Mondale participated.

Another crisis was the sarin gas attack in the Tokyo subway system that nearly cost thousands of lives and risked the lives of a couple of Americans who were on the affected cars. The embassy immediately assembled a task force and offered to send specialists from the United States to help advise on how to deal with people exposed to sarin gas. And there was coordination between American and Japanese police about this incident.

Then there was the rape of a 12-year-old girl in Okinawa by American Marines. Ambassador Mondale didn't wait for instructions from Washington. He faced the media immediately and apologized. That had a positive impact on what was clearly going to become a tough issue for the United States and the American Embassy. Indeed, it quickly led to a major challenge to the presence of U.S. forces in Okinawa. Working with the Japanese foreign ministry and defense forces, Mondale had to organize, within the embassy and with the American forces, an effort to move quickly to assuage legitimate concerns, to reduce anger, and to make some changes in the workings of the criminal process affecting American forces in Japan. The U.S. armed forces and the embassy made voluntary contributions to the family and the girl to show that America cared and wanted to deal with the terrible event in a responsible way.

Ambassador Mondale and the embassy worked closely with Washington to manage all these crises, but the initiative was always in the hands of the Tokyo embassy. Immediate reactions on the scene were essential in ameliorating the worst effects on the victims and on our relations with Japan.

All Crises Are Local

The above accounts are only a small selection of the many kinds of crises that our diplomats serving abroad have had to cope with in recent decades. The reader interested in learning more about diplomatic crisis management might wish to consult *Embassies Under Siege: Personal Accounts by Diplomats on the Front Line*, edited by Joseph G. Sullivan (Brassey's, 1995), which covers crises of recent years in Uganda, Iran, Afghanistan, Pakistan, Lebanon, El Salvador, and Kuwait (in addition to Liberia and Somalia).

Political pundits in the media are fond of quoting the dictum of former House Speaker Tip O'Neill that "all politics is local." The accounts in this chapter illustrate that in diplomatic work, "all crises are local." By their very nature they cannot be handled from Washington. Without an embassy on or near the scene of the crisis, the United States would be powerless to engage in whatever action is called for: protection of American people, property, and interests, humanitarian relief, technical assistance, public support, or in extremis mobilization of our available military forces and materiel to assist local efforts to cope with a disaster. Washington can provide policy guidance and when necessary money to meet essential needs. It is illustrative of the imperative of speedy action by those on the scene that in the latter case ambassadors are authorized to request from the aid agency in Washington a sum of up to $25,000 to provide local authorities with immediate disaster assistance. What is astonishing is that this figure is so embarrassingly small, coming as it does from the richest country in the world, and that the figure has not changed for decades.

Admittedly, many of the worst crises that our embassies have to deal with are terrorist attacks against our diplomatic installations and personnel serving abroad. One could argue that if we didn't have embassies and consulates in foreign countries, there would be an absence of official targets for terrorists to strike against. But that would not eliminate or even inhibit terrorist actions directed against the interests of the United States. Frustrated terrorists would simply redirect their attacks to nonofficial American targets abroad, whether businesses, schools, missions, aircraft and ships, resident American citizens, or even transient tourists, as already happens in some places these days. When terrorists find official premises that are too well protected (most are as yet not well enough protected), they bomb or otherwise attack other installations that symbolize America (such as a McDonald's), take American citizens hostage, or even kill people with no connection with the U.S. government simply because they are Americans and are vulnerable.

Foreign crises of various kinds will always be with us, for we cannot disengage from the world and withdraw behind our own borders. With the dispersion of our population outside our own country, the world has grown smaller. Americans are everywhere, and without our diplomatic and consular establishments throughout the world our citizens would be much more "on their own" than they are today. That is a reality from which there is no turning back.

Supporting Business Interests

O ne of the major functions of American diplomacy throughout our history, and certainly for the past century, has been to promote the economic welfare of the United States. Our country was somewhat hampered in earlier times by our own protectionist policies and high tariff regimes designed to protect nascent American industries from import competition. In the past 25 years the job of helping American business interests abroad has grown in importance because of a number of trends, including the globalization of our and other nations' economies, the growth of huge multinational companies, the increasing share of trade, and in particular exports, in our gross domestic product, and the shift from classic "smokestack" industries to high-technology and service companies needing worldwide markets as the dynamic leading edge of our economy.

While low-tech exports such as agricultural products and basic commodities like coal remain important in our export trade, increasingly we must compete with other industrialized countries, mostly in Europe and East Asia (led by Japan), in markets for high-tech goods. We suffer from two handicaps in this competition. One is that we have adopted stringent domestic laws against corrupt practices by our companies in promoting sales abroad—prohibiting bribery, kickbacks, price fixing, and sweetheart deals—and these are enforced with high criminal penalties that appear to be effective. We have tried, with limited success, to get competitor nations to adopt similar penalties for their companies engaging in foreign transactions, but the practices we have outlawed continue to exist elsewhere and to interfere with open and fair competition. We have encouraged importing nations to insist on transparency in contracting and purchasing in both the public and private sectors, again with limited success. One of the goals of U.S. diplomacy is to keep pressing other governments to cooperate in insisting on fairness and openness in commercial relations. Another problem is the unwillingness or inability of foreign governments to prevent the pirating of American intellectual property: software, music, videos, movies, and other patented and copyrighted material.

The other handicap is that our economy is so large and our companies so numerous that in many cases two, three, four, or more American companies are in competition with each other abroad, whereas countries with smaller economies have only one company in competition for the same business. As a result, the British, French, Italian, Japanese, or German embassy can go all out to support its company in the competition—and they do exactly that—whereas an American ambassador cannot favor one American company over another in trying to assist the American side. He must be completely evenhanded in his support of the American candidates. His best tactic is to insist that the American suitors be treated fairly, that the process be as open and transparent as possible, and that no corruption be present.

Economic and Commercial Diplomacy

Richard Gardner says that economic and commercial diplomacy will continue to be a critical part of the work of U.S. ambassadors, certainly equal in importance to more traditional diplomacy focused on political and security issues. The reasons for this are obvious: the end of the Cold War, the growing importance of foreign markets for U.S. industry and agriculture, and the aggressive intervention of other governments in support of foreign competitors of U.S. companies. Gardner served as the U.S. ambassador at two of what he facetiously describes as "hardship posts": Rome in the Carter administration and Madrid in the first Clinton administration. He says the contrast between those two experiences was dramatic.

In his four years in Italy, from 1977 to 1981, Gardner's principal focus was trying to keep the Italian Communists out of the government and dealing with NATO's deployment of cruise missiles as a counterweight to the Soviet SS-20s. The Communists were kept out of the government for four years, but ironically the man who was then the head of the Communist Youth League became in 1998 the prime minister of Italy. And the ambassador's Italian son-in-law became the prime minister's diplomatic adviser.

Spain

In Spain in the 1990s, in contrast to Italy in the 1970s, one of Gardner's major priorities was economic and commercial diplomacy. He makes a distinction between the two. Economic diplomacy, which is of great importance to American business, involves advocacy and negotiation on economic policy questions, many of them before international institutions like the World Trade Organization, the General Agreement on Tariffs and Trade, the European Union, and other regional economic organizations. Commercial diplomacy entails promoting specific transactions for American businessmen. Economic diplomacy is mainly the function of State Department officers, while officers of the Foreign Commercial Service of the Department of Commerce assigned to our embassies are also involved with commercial diplomacy.

What's more, economic diplomacy is mainly multilateral and regional, whereas commercial diplomacy is bilateral and concerns the country of the ambassador's assignment. This is particularly true for our major European embassies. More and more decision making on economic policy questions is done in Brussels, the headquarters of the European Union, and ambassadors accredited to the various EU countries have to intervene in their capitals to try to affect decisions being made in Brussels.

Gardner estimates that in contrast with his service in Italy 20 years earlier, at least one-third of his time in Madrid was devoted to economic and commercial diplomacy. An additional one-third was devoted to issues like NATO enlargement, Bosnia, the Middle East, and the Persian Gulf. The remaining one-third was divided between public diplomacy and embassy management.

As an example of regional economic diplomacy, Gardner cites his experience in Spain, which assumed the rotating presidency of the European Union for the last six months of 1995. Some months prior to that, Prime Minister Felipe Gonzalez and Foreign Minister Javier Solana made an approach to Gardner, saying their country took the presidency only once every six or seven years and that they wanted to do something historic as a relatively new member of the EU, not only to advance the cause of European unity but to promote Atlantic unity by bringing the United States and Europe closer together. There was the danger that, after the Cold War, Europe would turn inward toward internal matters and the United States would also look more to its domestic concerns.

At the same time Stuart Eizenstat, the U.S. representative to the EU in Brussels, was working with his colleagues there on a similar idea to use the six-month presidency of Spain to do something special. The outcome was the New Transatlantic Agenda document, which was signed in Madrid by President Clinton, EU President Jacques Santer, and Prime Minister Gonzalez in December 1995. Although it is easy to be skeptical about such documents, Gardner believes it changed in fundamental ways the institutional relationship between the United States and the EU, laying the basis for much closer cooperation between the two sides across the board—in political, economic, and transnational issues like the environment and nuclear proliferation and in cultural affairs. It provided for joint support of multilateral trade liberalization and for substantial dismantling of regulatory barriers to trade.

Gardner felt so strongly about this regional and multilateral focus that as ambassador to Spain he did something he had done earlier as ambassador to Italy, organizing a caucus of American ambassadors at our major European posts—in Britain, France, Germany, Italy, and Spain—and our ambassadors to NATO and to the European Union. They met every few months and found that they were all dealing with the same security, political, and economic issues. In the economic arena there were such subjects as motion pictures, bioengineered foods, and hormone-treated beef. These may sound esoteric, but they are very important to our export industries, and the need to fend off unjustified protectionist measures by the Europeans (usually initiated by France) was imperative.

In bilateral commercial diplomacy, the Madrid embassy was frequently called upon by individual U.S. firms to resolve a particular problem with the Spanish government. For example, the embassy helped the U.S. motion picture industry ease a dubbing license requirement that would have significantly reduced Hollywood's share of the Spanish motion picture market. (Its share was already 80 percent, but that wasn't enough for Jack Valenti, the head of the Motion Picture Association.) The embassy also lobbied hard with the ministries of economy and justice for better enforcement of intellectual property protection on behalf of U.S. computer software and pharmaceuticals.

In two important examples of commercial diplomacy, the embassy was called on to help U.S. suppliers of military equipment in head-to-head contests with European competitors. The Sikorsky Aircraft Corporation, a division of United Technologies, asked for embassy help in securing a level playing field in its competition with the French-German Eurocopter consortium for the sale of helicopters to the Spanish army. In support of Sikorsky's Black Hawk helicopters, involving at least a quarter of a billion dollars of revenue and hundreds of U.S. jobs, the ambassador not only mobilized a dozen members of his staff but devoted many hours personally to meetings with key Spanish ministers, under secretaries, and senior military officers. He also obtained letters of support from top officials of our executive branch.

Ambassador Gardner also did something a bit unusual that he

thought might be effective. He came across a clipping from a French newspaper reporting that a French farmer had become exasperated with one of the French-German-built military helicopters that had been flying over his land. The farmer's irritation had got the better of him, and he had picked up a rifle and with one shot brought that helicopter down. Gardner's deputy in the embassy at the time told him that he had flown the American Black Hawk in the Grenada operation and although it had been hit three or four times by antiaircraft fire it had survived. Gardner knew that the king of Spain was a helicopter pilot. The king's son, the prince of Asturias, who had been a student at Georgetown University in Washington, was having dinner with the ambassador. Gardner slipped him the clipping and suggested he show it to his father, as it might interest him as a helicopter pilot.

This effort was a good try, but the French government was equally active in promoting the French-German product, not only with pressure from the French ambassador but with personal telephone calls from President Jacques Chirac to Prime Minister Gonzalez. According to the Spanish press, Chirac threatened not only to withhold support from Spain on key issues before the European Union but also to refuse extradition of Basque terrorists. Despite the clear preference of the ministry of defense for the Sikorsky helicopters, the Spanish government finally chose the French-German aircraft instead.

The Madrid embassy obtained a better result in a second major U.S. sale: an $800 million contract with the Spanish navy for Lockheed Martin's Aegis naval combat system. Here again the U.S. equipment was clearly superior to the French-German alternative. This time European political pressure could not overcome the U.S. technological advantages because the European system was still on the drawing board and could not possibly be ready in time to meet Spain's requirements.

Gardner emphasizes that the role of the embassy in these two transactions was not just in lobbying the Spanish government but in advising the American companies on how to formulate their proposals in a way most likely to be persuasive. This meant building in a substantial element of Spanish coproduction and research and development so that the industry ministry as well as the defense ministry could make the case for the U.S. product.

Ambassador Gardner thinks the role of American embassies in economic and commercial diplomacy is destined to grow in importance, particularly in Europe. In the years ahead members of the European Union will be focusing on vital questions such as the Euro, the EU budget, the

Common Agricultural Policy, enlargement of the EU, and consequent changes in EU decision making and institutional arrangements. Europe will also be developing an integrated defense industry and some kind of independent defense and security identity. In this political environment, it will require extremely vigorous and intelligent action by our embassies to protect U.S. economic and commercial interests.

Problem Solving in Kenya

Elinor Constable served as ambassador to the East African country of Kenya from 1986 to 1989. A specialist in economic affairs, she did not need to be reminded by the State Department that one of the most important responsibilities of an American ambassador is to promote two-way trade and to assist American companies doing business with or in the host country. On her arrival in Nairobi she set as one of her major goals to improve the investment and operating climate in Kenya.

But that proved to be an uphill struggle. Kenya was in a long, slow, steady economic decline. The investment climate had deteriorated drastically, corruption was endemic, and U.S. investment there was declining. Earlier Kenya had been a star performer, with apparent political stability, relatively sound macroeconomic policies, a thriving private sector, a healthy agricultural sector, and good growth rates. It was one of the few countries in Africa that had never had to reschedule its debt. However, a combination of a record-high population growth rate, state interference in the market, slowing investment, crony capitalism, and widespread corruption had put investors and business people in a generally negative mood. Companies already operating there encountered arbitrary limits on remittance of profits, dividends, and royalties, other forms of red tape and bureaucratic inefficiency, vague price controls, and unreasonable restrictions on employment of expatriates. The word was spreading that Kenya was no longer a good place to do business.

It was not that Kenya's political leadership disliked foreign investment. On the contrary, they were hoping that new economic sanctions recently imposed on South Africa would stimulate American companies to relocate from South Africa to other places on the continent like Kenya. Secretary of State Shultz paid a visit to Nairobi shortly after Ambassador Constable's arrival, and in the obligatory meeting with President Moi, who had ruled Kenya since 1978, Moi asked Shultz to urge American companies to relocate to Kenya. The secretary's response was that that was the job of President Moi and his colleagues in the Kenyan government. Constable was of the same view, and she notes that the kind of pressure Moi wanted the U.S. government to exert is not only inappropriate but doesn't work. It was up to the Kenyans to change the business climate. The ambassador made clear to her Kenyan interlocutors that she would not declare that Kenya was a fine place to do business until that was true.

Constable set to work on the problems being experienced by American companies in Kenya by preparing what diplomats call a "nonpaper" (a simple piece of paper with no letterhead, signature, or other attribute that would identify its origin), in which she listed a dozen or so specific problems that individual American companies were having. One of the most bizarre involved the cancellation of the radio permit of a flower exporter in northern Kenya who, because of unreliable standard means of communication, had resorted to handling all orders by shortwave radio. The license revocation was justified on the grounds that the radio was allegedly being used to foment political opposition to Moi. Constable eventually took this preposterous situation directly to President Moi, but the license was still not restored.

She delivered her nonpaper to the senior civil servant in the economics ministry, an able and serious person who she thought could help with the bureaucracy in resolving some of these problems. The man read the list and then remarked that she had left something out. Asked what that was, he candidly replied: "Corruption!" She said she was certainly aware of that problem, but no American ambassador was going to put that in writing, even in a nonpaper.

Constable's staff did an analysis of the corruption problem, which produced some interesting conclusions. Corruption had certainly been significant under the regime of Moi's predecessor as president, Jomo Kenyatta, who ruled from independence in 1962 until 1978, but all during his tenure foreign investment continued to grow. What had changed? Kenyatta's people had skimmed off the top, taking a constant share of a growing economic pie. By the mid-80s, on the other hand, projects and proposals had become so riddled with required payoffs that they were uneconomic. Corruption was eating up a growing share of a shrinking pie. Population pressures and shifting tribal pre-eminence were important causes of the change, but greed seemed to have simply gotten out of control.

One particular episode highlights the critical role of an ambassador in this discouraging environment. A U.S. company came to the embassy seeking help. The Kenyan government had decided to "Kenyanize" its sector of the economy, so the company negotiated with Kenyan officials the terms under which the operation would become majority Kenyan owned, with the U.S. company retaining an important minority interest. The negotiations went well from the American point of view, and a final deal had been agreed to, but on the day set for formal signature the Kenyans balked and then stonewalled.

A key player on the Kenyan side was a senior minister who, in response to the ambassador's appeal, said he knew nothing about the situation but promised to look into it. The truth was that this minister had been calling the shots for the Kenyan side. One report had him sitting in an adjoining room during the discussions. It was well known in Nairobi that the Kenyans had reneged on the deal because that minister had decided that his personal payoff was not large enough.

The stonewalling continued for some months until someone well connected in Washington who knew the story persuaded Commerce Secretary Malcolm Baldrige to write a scathing letter to President Moi accusing the minister of corruption in this case. The letter was sent to Ambassador Constable with instructions that she deliver it to President Moi personally. She wisely concluded that that would be a very bad idea, so she sat on the letter and bided her time. An ambassador cannot exactly ignore such an instruction, or refuse to carry it out, but she can amend it or adapt it.

She kept receiving messages from Commerce asking if she had delivered the letter and eventually got a desperate phone call from an old friend at Commerce who was being pressured to prod Constable in Nairobi. She told the friend that she would "sort of deliver it, but not to President Moi," and her friend could tell her bosses at Commerce that the letter was being delivered.

As she had been planning, Constable took the letter to the senior minister accused in the letter and said to him: "I have this letter from Washington that I'm supposed to deliver to the president, and I don't think I want to do that. But I'm going to let you read it." The minister read it and exploded with outrage. "I'm not a crook," he said. "I didn't say you were a crook," the ambassador replied. "Yes, but this letter says I'm a crook," said the minister. Then the ambassador said: "Well, I didn't write the letter. I'm not even delivering the letter. But you need to know what people in Washington are saying about you."

The minister continued to fuss and fume. Constable took back the letter, put it in her pocket, and said: "Look, why don't you just cut this deal so that people won't say these terrible things about you, and all this will be history." Two days later the deal was signed.

Looking back on her tour in Nairobi, the ambassador was pleased that a number of small problems for American companies had been solved. They were able to get their money out; they were again able to hire expatriates; they obtained some permits. But with the larger problems, she concluded, unless there is sufficient motivation at the top of the host country's government to put things right, there isn't much an American ambassador can do. Unfortunately, the underlying problems were never addressed, investment continued to decline, and her last speech in Nairobi was about the reasons for that decline.

What must also be stressed, however, is that without an ambassador resident in Nairobi, the unfortunately phrased letter from Secretary Baldrige to President Moi would have been delivered as planned by Washington, not as modified by Constable in Kenya. She knew how to use the letter to accomplish the objective of getting the deal signed, rather than simply to antagonize the big men at the top of the Kenyan government, who would have ignored it if not worse. What Ambassador Constable employed was diplomacy, and in the only venue—on the ground in Kenya—where it could be effective.

Deepening Commercial Relations With Mexico

Former congressman and stock exchange president James R. Jones was our ambassador to Mexico in the first Clinton administration.* On his arrival in Mexico City in 1993 he established six major objectives for the embassy to work on during his tour. At the top of the list was commerce: to broaden and deepen the commercial relationship between the United States and Mexico. The embassy's shorthand description of that goal was simply "to help U.S. business do business with Mexico."

Jones is convinced that in the post-Cold War era this commercial function will continue to grow in importance at every American Embassy. Global competition is likely to be more commercial than military in the 21st century, and most economic growth will occur in the markets of the developing world. Thus if our goal is to continue to expand economic opportunities for future generations of Americans, we must use every tool available to open these developing markets to U.S. goods and services.

Jones believes that expanding commerce is also one of the most effective diplomatic tools we have for advancing American values around the

---

* He represented the first district of Oklahoma in the U.S. Congress from 1972 to 1986 and also served as president of the American Stock Exchange in New York, 1989-93.

world. For example, in 1994 the Mexican government faced an insurrection in its southern state of Chiapas. A decision under consideration to suppress the rebellion with traditional methods would have engendered major human rights problems. While it was important for the ambassador to communicate his own government's view on the situation, in meetings with the president of Mexico and other senior officials, the most effective argument he had available was to stress the adverse impact such an action would have on bilateral commerce and U.S. investment in Mexico. The Mexican government wisely decided to try to resolve this conflict through political dialogue rather than traditional military suppression.

Expanded commerce also has a major indirect effect in spreading American values, the ambassador argues. Practitioners of the "crony capitalism" that exists in much of the developing world soon learn that certain practices are unacceptable, and sometimes even illegal, when dealing with U.S. business enterprises. To work with American companies, they must adopt new accounting principles, and transparency in business dealings must become the norm. Such changes inspire confidence among many of the people left out of the weak economies in developing countries and produce pressure and demands for similar transparency and fair dealing in other domains, such as political and democratic institutions and practices.

How did the embassy in Mexico City implement the objective of expanding commercial relations? It required a team approach involving all sections of the embassy. While the officers of the Foreign Commercial Service generally took the lead, all 33 U.S. government agencies represented in the embassy—from the military, law enforcement, and intelligence staffs to the agriculture and economic staffs—were expected to be active players on the commercial team.

As nations convert to market economies, increased privatization of government enterprises and additional public bidding for government contracts offer new opportunities for American firms. In Mexico the embassy became an active partner of U.S. firms bidding on government contracts or investing in privatized enterprises. By including all parts of the embassy it was possible to learn in a timely fashion about these new opportunities, enabling them to be analyzed and the appropriate American business sector alerted.

In at least two instances the embassy's direct oversight revealed that the bidding processes were less than transparent, to the detriment of U.S. bidders. The embassy's immediate intervention overturned those bid awards and established a new round of bidding. Once the playing field had been leveled, American firms won the bids.

Another area the embassy emphasized was helping midsize and small American firms compete in Mexico. Large multinational companies have deep pockets to pay for market analysis and the establishment of business contacts. Most smaller firms shy away from trying to expand their business abroad because they are unfamiliar with the markets, have no contacts, and simply cannot afford the trial-and-error financial losses that accompany learning from experience outside the United States. The embassy's program of preparing on-the-shelf market surveys of the most promising Mexican economic sectors, coupled with its detailed briefings on the business climate and practices and its ability to introduce U.S. firms to potential Mexican joint venture partners, benefited the American medium-size business sector enormously.

On a daily basis, the embassy identified economic opportunities in Mexico and communicated that information back to the United States. On average once a week, the embassy hosted an American trade delegation. Among the services provided to visitors were general or tailored market surveys, briefings on how to conduct business in Mexico, and identifying and arranging appointments with potential Mexican customers, distributors, or joint venture partners.

Members of the embassy team, including the ambassador on many occasions, accompanied the visiting business groups to these meetings to lend support and credibility to their marketing efforts. The ambassador regularly hosted receptions or dinners at his residence at which business leaders from both countries could develop social and personal relationships and from which much business flowed.

Finally, the embassy played an important role in bilateral efforts to implement NAFTA (the North American Free Trade Agreement) and break down barriers to open markets. Jones points out that there is a natural tendency in every country to protect its own industries from foreign competition. As a result of carefully cultivated professional and personal relationships with officials in every part of the Mexican government, the embassy overcame virtually all pockets of bureaucratic resistance to implementation of NAFTA.

To be successful, Jones says, "all these efforts require a savvy, committed, tuned-in embassy team, in country, doing the research, making the contacts, listening for ideas and trends. No American multinational firm would dream of conducting its business in any foreign country from its headquarters in the United States. Neither should the United States government."

The proof is in the results, he insists. In his four years as ambassador, both U.S exports to Mexico and total bilateral trade more than doubled. Exports increased from $41 billion to over $80 billion. In 1998 Mexico surpassed Japan as America's second largest export market and trading partner.

Searching for Opportunities in Malaysia

When John S. Wolf arrived in Kuala Lumpur in 1992 as the American ambassador to Malaysia, he found that economic ties with that nation were in one sense quite robust. Malaysia was the United States' 19th largest trading partner, with nearly $7 billion of U.S. investment, predominantly in upstream petroleum activities and in electronics. However, political relations between Washington and Kuala Lumpur were frosty, with the result that American firms were not penetrating new sectors and were generally not competitive in bidding for new infrastructure projects, for example in power generation and the construction of the new $4 billion Kuala Lumpur airport.

Wolf told his country team that the thematic mantra he wanted every embassy employee to project was "America is worthy to be a friend and is uniquely able to exercise leadership worldwide." He wanted his colleagues to eschew the role of problem solver that so often is the perceived mission of our embassies. Instead, he wanted everyone to focus on opportunities, identifying them and making them happen. Focusing primarily on problems, he felt, meant that one constantly looked for problems to solve, and when there were none, one virtually created them. A focus on opportunities had the potential "to redefine the bilateral geography," to make clear to decision makers in Kuala Lumpur and Washington, and to CEOs in business centers around America, that there existed real win-win possibilities that made resolution of impediments much easier to accomplish.

In December 1992 there appeared on the scene a textbook opportunity: initiation of an accelerated effort to sell American military aircraft to Malaysia in competition with Russia. For nearly a dozen years, Malaysia had been shopping, but American analysts in the public and private sectors had concluded that Malaysia was unlikely to become a buyer. The sterile official dialogue meant that this issue was far off policy radars.

Announcements in Kuala Lumpur and Moscow indicated that a sale by Russia was nevertheless imminent. Ambassador Wolf arranged for Malaysia's minister of defense to visit the aircraft carrier Kitty Hawk, fortuitously in transit to the Persian Gulf, to demonstrate U.S. aircraft capabilities and to elicit definitive word about the announced sale. The minister confirmed Malaysia's intention to buy from the Russians and explained that the reason the United States was not competitive was that we had taken Malaysia for granted, that U.S. officials were unresponsive, and that our languid official approach was matched in the private sector. Whether because of euphoria induced by the flight to and from the carrier or, more likely, the realization that the United States had a superior product with greater potential benefits for Malaysia, the minister agreed to give the Americans a short window in which to make their best offer.

By calling personally the heads of McDonnell Douglas (maker of the F-18), General Dynamics (maker of the F-16), and the Defense Security Assistance Agency, Ambassador Wolf was able to stimulate an urgent effort by the government and the potential suppliers to develop price and availability (P&A) information, to obtain a letter of support from the secretary of defense, and to field teams to present the P&A data to the Malaysians. It was important that McDonnell Douglas's team was headed by its CEO and that our military services sent flag officers. This effort took less than seven weeks. It was enough to give the American offer a hearing and then a chance to compete head to head with the Russian offer. During the following months the companies and the U.S. government worked intensively on issues such as weapons releasability, costing, financing, and offset arrangements.

By mid-March Malaysia short-listed the Russian MIG and the U.S. F/A-18 Hornet. At that point the embassy decided to put its full lobbying effort behind McDonnell Douglas, even though Lockheed (which had acquired the F-16 division from General Dynamics) insisted it was still a contender. The question of which U.S. company to back in this case was relatively straightforward, but such questions are becoming increasingly difficult as globalization blurs national and corporate identities. Wolf met with Lockheed's CEO to discuss the issue, and the CEO agreed with Wolf's reasons for giving full support to McDonnell Douglas, with the understanding that if Lockheed were to be added to the Malaysian short-list, the embassy would give that company equal support.

Just under a year from the commencement of the sales effort, the Malaysian government signed a letter of acceptance with the U.S. Navy to buy eight F/A-18 aircraft worth $700 million—and nearly 15,000 U.S. jobs. The successful outcome resulted from a true team effort, with the public and private sectors working together on a daily basis to share information, critique progress, and hone tactics. The ambassador was personally involved, working through both official channels and informal networks to open doors and speed decision making.

The F/A-18 deal put Malaysia back on the map, not just in Washington but in corporate board rooms around the country. A security relationship with Malaysia was established that will endure many years into the future, and that led to the signing of a logistics agreement that has made it easier for U.S. forces to operate far from their home bases. U.S.-Malaysian industry ties were strengthened, jobs created, and strategic opportunities enhanced. With active embassy involvement there followed U.S. investments in Malaysia's burgeoning power-generating sector and a rollback of Malaysian product quotas on plastics input imports.

Robust economic growth in Southeast Asia in the early 1990s brought a rapid increase in business visitors to Malaysia. In counseling them the embassy made five points based on what had been learned from the aircraft sale:

1. Face to face beats fax to fax. Americans needed to network better and to build the personal relationships that are fundamental to business success in Asia.

2. Price, quality, and timeliness matter, as does careful regard for the specifications in bids. Too often in sales, items are included that make American prices appear to be higher than their competitors'.

3. In Malaysia one could not "just sell a piece of metal." Bids were evaluated not only for the immediate benefit but for the impact a partnership could have on Malaysia's quest for its Vision 2020—a fully developed economy by that year.

4. CEOs like to speak to CEOs. While regional executives can often get high-level audiences, only the top corporate officials have the stature to validate the approach outlined above. The Malaysians saw in their nearly $20 billion in trade with the United States more than enough reason to be treated as a key market. In fact the United States exported more to Malaysia than to Indonesia, India, Russia, or all of Eastern Europe combined. Yet until 1993 it was rarely visited by corporate jets.

5. Doing business in Asia requires patience. Over a three-year period Hughes Corporation submitted more than 30 contract revisions in its attempt to secure a satellite contract—and in the end succeeded. Triton Energy took 23 years to win the agreement of Thailand and Malaysia to develop resources in disputed offshore territory. Today's estimates of the size of the gas reserves show it was worth the wait.

Opening doors for visiting business people was only half the embassy's efforts on behalf of commerce. The other half was reaching out to business people in the United States. There is an annual tour of the United States by American ambassadors serving in the ASEAN (Association of Southeast Asian Nations) countries, and the Commerce Department hosts an annual Pacific Roundtable. Ambassador Wolf used his trips home to visit different corporate centers and develop personal relationships with top-level officials, and then kept in touch with them by fax and e-mail.

Back in Kuala Lumpur the continuing dialogue with Malaysian officials went beyond individual projects to focus on such matters as enhancing intellectual property protection, addressing concerns about work permits, improving customs procedures, and making the electric grid more reliable. The economic decision makers the embassy sought to influence were the same members of the host country's public/private power elite with whom the embassy interacted on other issues as wide ranging as narcotics interdiction, nuclear nonproliferation, and governmental institutional reform. Advancing American commercial interests was thus intertwined with promoting our overall national security concerns in the context of a new and positive bilateral relationship with a key country in Southeast Asia.

Dealing With Expropriation in Venezuela

A senior specialist in diplomacy with Latin America, Harry W. Shlaudeman headed the U.S. Embassy in Caracas, Venezuela, when that country nationalized its important petroleum industry.*

Ever since Lazaro Cardenas nationalized the Mexican petroleum industry in 1938, expropriation of foreign direct investment in Latin America has been a recurring problem in U.S. relations with that region. The Peruvian government's seizure 30 years later of the assets of the International Petroleum Company (a Canadian subsidiary of Exxon) was the first in a series of particularly contentious expropriation cases culminating in the 1975-76 nationalization of Venezuela's huge oil industry. All of these cases brought U.S. standards for the treatment of private investment and property rights into conflict with the intense economic nationalism so prevalent in Latin America. And in all of them, other Latin American governments uniformly supported the expropriating power.

---

* He also served as ambassador to Peru, Argentina, Brazil, and Nicaragua, as assistant secretary of state for inter-American affairs, and as ambassador at large.

In response to Salvador Allende's 1970 expropriation of the U.S. copper companies in Chile, the Nixon administration issued a formal White House statement reiterating and refining U.S. policy on the issue. The statement reinforced legislation already on the books, particularly the Hickenlooper and Gonzales amendments to the Foreign Assistance Act. The purpose of such legislation was to deny foreign aid (Hickenlooper) and U.S. support in the international financial institutions (Gonzales) when expropriation took place without compensation. As defined in the Nixon statement, compensation in such cases would have to be "prompt, adequate and effective." (To all intents "effective" meant spendable.)

The Venezuelan case came with that backdrop. It was far larger in monetary terms than the others and of considerably greater economic importance to the United States. It probably remains to this day the largest expropriation of U.S. private investment in history. As an example of its scope, Creole, the Exxon subsidiary, at one time was alone taking 2 million barrels of oil a day out of Lake Maracaibo. The Venezuelan expropriation took place in the wake of the first oil shock that erupted from the Middle East and at a time of unprecedented high oil prices. That context sharpened in most sectors of Venezuelan society the long-standing sentiment favoring nationalization. Few Venezuelans appreciated the critical contributions the U.S. companies had made, such as Standard Oil of New Jersey's development of the technology that made it possible to extract oil from the bottom of Lake Maracaibo.

Carlos Andres Perez made it clear in his winning 1974 campaign for the presidency that he would move to nationalize the petroleum industry. When Ambassador Shlaudeman arrived in Caracas in May 1975, a legislative proposal to that end was already taking shape. Beyond existing policy, he had no instructions for dealing with this momentous development. Washington seemed to be waiting to see how the Venezuelans would deal with the question of compensation, hoping that the previous nationalization of an American company's iron-mining interests would provide a precedent. In that case informal talks with the company had led to an agreed solution. But the embassy soon concluded, and reported to the Department of State, that this time there would be no substantive talks with the companies and no agreement, cosmetic or otherwise.

It also became evident before long that there was no consensus in Washington on how to proceed. On one hand Venezuela was a critical source of petroleum supply at a time when the first oil shock was still reverberating. We could not ignore the fact that the country's shipments had continued throughout the Arab embargo, demonstrating the relia-bility of that source. On the other hand, U.S. policy to require compen-sation and to act in its absence was clear. Other governments and investors would be watching closely to judge the consistency of our own policy pronouncements. The Venezuelan case could establish a damag-ing precedent.

As it emerged in its final form, the Venezuelan legislation tended to reinforce that fear. There was to be no compensation for the concessions, only a so-called compensation fund to pay for installations and equip-ment after settlement of tax obligations and deductions for defective equipment. In this there was an ominous echo of a similar provision in the Chilean copper nationalization. The Allende regime ultimately deter-mined that the companies owed more than the value of what they had left behind. Finally, the new national petroleum entity, Petroleos de Venezuela-Petroven, would offer the companies technical service con-tracts of 15 cents a barrel for a period of time to be determined.

Shlaudeman and his embassy colleagues spent considerable time and effort sounding out Venezuelans across the spectrum on the issue and examining it carefully from every aspect of U.S. interests. They concluded that it was almost impossible to exaggerate the importance of how the U.S. government would decide to react to the nationalization. In a series of telegrams to Washington Shlaudeman emphasized how strong senti-ment favoring economic nationalization was in Venezuela, to the point that support for unilateral nationalization was virtually universal. Nothing that the U.S. government might say or do would impede the process or improve its terms. But a hostile or even critical response could do severe damage to our position in the country.

The Caracas embassy believed that the U.S.-Venezuelan relationship itself was of overriding importance, that the objective should be to main-tain a strong and cooperative relationship of a kind that would support Venezuela's role as a reliable source of oil, as a leading democracy in Latin America, and as a helpful ally on the international scene. The embassy argued with regard to compensation that the technical service contracts could, if the companies decided to accept them, meet the requirements of our policy. And the anticipation was that given an ami-cable resolution of the nationalization, there would be openings in the future for the companies to return, in particular to provide technology for the development of the heavy oil in the massive Orinoco Tar Belt.

In Washington the State Department's Bureau of Inter-American Affairs strongly supported the position of the embassy in Caracas. The department's legal adviser and his staff just as strongly opposed it. They argued that the service contracts could not be considered either "adequate" or "prompt" compensation and that existing policy and the national interest in preventing a damaging precedent made it necessary for the U.S. government to issue a formal protest, espouse claims, and, in appropriate circumstances, consider application of the restrictive amendments in our foreign assistance legislation. Other bureaus in State and other departments in the Ford administration took no position initially, weighing the arguments as they emerged. The companies too for the most part kept their own counsel, convinced no doubt that expropriation was inevitable and reluctant to do anything that might adversely affect their dealings with OPEC (the Organization of Petroleum Exporting Countries).

After a lengthy dialogue with the Department of State on the issue, Ambassador Shlaudeman was asked to return to Washington to defend his position at a large meeting convoked by the deputy secretary of state. He was able in that meeting to convey a firsthand sense of the passions nationalization had aroused in Venezuela and the importance to the future of the relationship of a measured response on our part. The deputy legal adviser forcefully made the arguments on the other side. As is often the outcome on such occasions, no formal decision emerged from the meeting but it was generally understood that the embassy's position had prevailed. The United States issued no protest, espoused no claims, and applied no restrictive legislation to Venezuela. It is difficult to say what would have resulted if the embassy and Ambassador Shlaudeman had remained passive or adopted a different position. At the least, those in Washington who favored a nonassertive response would have found the going more difficult.

As it turned out, the service contracts provided some compensation to some companies. Others found them insufficiently profitable. A lengthy dispute over taxes reduced the value of the eventual payments from the so-called compensation fund. In time, passions subsided and Venezuelans began to look more closely at the country's self-interest. Petroven invited those companies with an interest in returning to bid on new concessions outside the old Maracaibo basin. In addition, several of the companies have, also by invitation, provided technological assistance in the effort to develop the Orinoco Tar Belt. And surprisingly, direct investment reversed direction with Petroven's purchase of the Citgo chain of service stations in the United States. Through all the intervening years the relationship between the two countries has remained close and cooperative, to the considerable benefit of the United States.

In contrast to the above episode, concern for the overall relationship did not prevent Ambassador Shlaudeman from making the strongest possible protest in another expropriation case during his tour in Caracas. The circumstances were quite different. Purported guerrillas kidnapped the representative of a nonpetroleum U.S. company and subsequently demanded the publication of a manifesto they had prepared. The company complied, placing the manifesto in a Miami newspaper despite President Perez's stern injunction against responding in any form to the kidnappers. He thereupon issued a decree expropriating the company's operations in Venezuela. Shlaudeman met with Perez immediately and told him his action was unjustified and unacceptable. Ultimately, Perez decided not to enforce the decree and the company continued in business in Venezuela.

One conclusion to be drawn from this account is that as important as it is to defend and promote our principles of correct international behavior, and to protect the interests of American companies that invest abroad, we must balance those serious concerns against other important national interests that may be severely damaged by a strict adherence to undifferentiated demands for recognition of property rights. Balancing these sometimes contradictory concerns requires intelligent, serious, and informed diplomacy, both in the field and in Washington, and clearly necessitates the full involvement of our embassies and ambassadors abroad.

Supporting America's Prosperity

Craig Johnstone, senior vice president at the U.S. Chamber of Commerce with experience heading a private plastics company, was a career Foreign Service officer who served as ambassador to Algeria in the second Reagan administration. In addressing the subject of the ambassadorial job of supporting American business abroad, he offers a critical examination of how well U.S. diplomacy is performing today and offers some thoughtful proposals for improving that performance.

Ensuring the nation's prosperity, Johnstone says, is one of the seven national interests defined in the U.S. International Affairs Strategic Plan, a document worked out meticulously between the White House and some 30 federal agencies and the U.S. Congress. The other six national interests are:

- protecting our national security;
- protecting citizens abroad and America's borders;
- fighting international crime;
- building democracies and upholding human rights;
- providing humanitarian relief; and
- ensuring a habitable world by addressing the interrelated problems of population growth, environmental degradation, and the spread of disease.

Although these seven national interests are not rank ordered, it is safe to say that promoting America's prosperity ranks high on the list. To an extent not widely recognized, the prosperity goal is critically important to the American people, whose economy is increasingly dependent on international trade. In the 1960s, imports and exports, added together, amounted to less than 10 percent of our gross national product. By the 1970s the percentage had moved into double digits, and by the 1980s it had crossed the 20 percent threshold. Today, imports added to exports come to 36 percent of our GNP. Exports have accounted for one-third of our economic growth in recent years, and our often-maligned imports have made a major contribution to the economy by keeping prices and inflation down. It is no exaggeration to say that the current economic boom is fueled directly or indirectly by international trade.

The U.S. economy's increased dependence on trade puts new and substantially greater responsibilities on the shoulders of our overseas embassies and ambassadors. Consider their role in achieving each of four strategic goals related primarily to U.S. prosperity.

Opening markets and ensuring free trade. Trade agreements don't just happen. They must be negotiated, and not only in trade rounds or in the World Trade Organization. They must be negotiated in capitals around the world by ambassadors and their staffs, relying on traditional skills of reporting and advocacy. Our embassies play a critical role in providing understanding of the trade positions of other countries, advocating our negotiating positions, and monitoring trade practices and compliance with agreements.

Increasing American exports and overseas investments. Ambassadors have long had commercial responsibilities, but the increased dependence of the U.S. economy on international trade lends a new sense of urgency to the promotion of U.S. exports, which are not just about money and profits but also about American jobs. The modern ambassador spends as much or more time promoting the nation's exports as on any geopolitical goal.

Ensuring stable but flexible international financial systems. If there is any lesson to be learned from the Asian financial crisis of 1997-98, it is that we need to be able to assess the strengths and weaknesses of financial institutions in all corners of the world. The weaknesses of core institutions in Thailand, in Indonesia, and in Japan were no secret to us. Yet we were caught by surprise when they combined to bring Asia's economic boom to a cataclysmic halt. Properly staffed, U.S. embassies and ambassadors provide the platform from which we can assess, analyze, and make recommendations on the courses of action required to keep financial markets and systems stable.

Promoting broad-based economic growth. Ambassadors also play a role in coordinating economic development programs and ensuring that they are consistent with and contribute to our foreign policy goals. During the Cold War economic development was an ancillary activity of American foreign policy. To put it bluntly, foreign aid was given to countries to buy their allegiance. The funds were then administered by the Agency for International Development to achieve developmental objectives. The State Department's role in development—and by extension the ambassador's role—often ended when the allegiances were bought. What AID did with the money, while important, was not critical to the central purpose of the assistance, winning the Cold War.

Today's economic development programs serve a number of quite different objectives, Johnstone points out, none more important than the promotion of U.S. prosperity. U.S. exports to the developing world are growing at a much faster pace than exports to the developed world. These new markets represent the future, and they must be helped to grow. For ambassadors, ensuring that economic development programs in developing countries actually serve U.S. national interests, particularly the prosperity interest, has moved from being an ancillary activity to center stage.

What skills will ambassadors need to be able to play the critical role they will be asked to assume in our new trade-dependent era? Are ambassadors and their embassies up to the task? In some respects the overseas diplomatic establishment is not fully prepared for the role it must play if America is to use its international reach on behalf of its own prosperity. Johnstone outlines some of the managerial skills that 21st-century ambassadors need to focus on (in addition to the job of communicating with the American people mentioned in chapter 1).

Management Skills

The nature of foreign policy in the 21st century will differ in substantial ways from the geopolitically intensive foreign policy of the Cold War period. During that time the core skills required were in the areas of reporting, analysis, and policy formulation. These will remain basic needs in the new century, but they will not be sufficient. The new era will require less policy formulation and more program implementation. What will be most essential are basic management skills—techniques for getting things done. In no field are these skills more necessary than in trade promotion. For ambassadors this will mean knowing how to:

- *Set clearly defined and measurable export goals.* No private-sector company embarks on a sales campaign without goals. Determining one's goals at the beginning of the process sets the parameters for the strategy and makes possible after-action evaluation. Historically, the "foreign affairs culture" has resisted goal setting. Goals seem simplistic and obvious, but the debate that ensues around every effort to set foreign policy goals, including export goals, belies this rationale. On the contrary, it is in the goal-setting phase that the discovery is often made that the various parts of an organization are not synchronized. In Algeria, for example, the commercial section of the embassy listed its goal as "serving the American business community [in Algeria]." This the staff did admirably but with little effect on U.S. exports. The problem was that U.S. business people did not come to Algeria. It was only after the goal was changed to "doubling exports" that the commercial section focused on its real task, selling the Algerian market to U.S. business.

- *Use all elements of the embassy,* not just the commercial section, to achieve success. Again using Algeria as an example, the junior political officer set the embassy on a course to land a billion-dollar pipeline contract, the U.S. Information Service public affairs officer sealed a deal for General Motors, and the economic officer stole a contract from the European Airbus consortium on behalf of Boeing.

- *Be aggressive, be innovative, and take risks.* There are very few sure things in program management, and certainly none in sales and trade promotion. The 21st-century ambassador will need to oppose the risk-averse culture of traditional diplomacy. The best deals for American business often come from low-probability, high-risk efforts. The Bechtel Corporation benefited from a rapprochement between Algeria and Morocco, two countries nearly in a state of war, and the rapprochement itself resulted from a low-probability idea generated by a junior officer in our Algiers embassy.

- *Assess progress against concrete criteria and revise courses of action accordingly.* Traditionally in the diplomatic establishment, once a course is set it is often left on autopilot. The same bad program can go on year after year without achieving results.
- *Motivate and lead.* In some respects ambassadorial leadership has become even more important in the post-Cold War era. Most of America's new goals must be achieved by programs, and programs are managed by the lower levels of an organization, not at the top.This contrasts with the policy-making paradigm of the Cold War. To run an organization that must implement its activities using its staff requires leadership, the alignment of goals, and clear communication.

The skills enumerated above, Johnstone concludes, are not unique to the export promotion function. They are critical to dealing with a host of new international responsibilities in areas as diverse as law enforcement and protection of the environment. Across the board, embassies and ambassadors are more important to the achievement of the nation's global objectives now than they were during the Cold War. Nowhere is this more true than in the promotion of America's prosperity.

Conclusion

The foregoing personal accounts of a spectrum of American ambassadors have provided evidence that embassies are neither obsolete nor dispensable but, rather, are just as essential as they have always been to the execution of our diplomacy around the world that protects and advances America's vital national interests.

Embassies—not just ambassadors but their highly capable staffs as well—play essential roles in assisting American citizens abroad. Ambassadors act as the leaders of the official and private American communities living and working in foreign countries, providing a direct link to their federal government at home. As the communicators and implementers of U.S. foreign policies, our diplomats tend to our bilateral relationships with all the other governments in the world, explaining our policies to foreign governments and peoples. At the same time, they provide our government in Washington with the most reliable understanding of events that occur in the countries where they are accredited, so that decisions and policies can be arrived at in Washington based on accurate information and credible analysis.

Embassies in foreign capitals are essential as well to deal with the various disruptions of stability and disasters—such as civil strife and violence, terrorist threats and actual attacks, and natural catastrophes such as earthquakes, floods, and volcanic eruptions—many of which occur without advance warning and are impossible to prepare for. Whatever the American role and possible actions in such situations turn out to be, the primary responsibility falls on U.S. officials on the scene. Our reactions cannot be masterminded from Washington because of the constraints of time and distance. Without embassies on the ground, America would be powerless to deal appropriately with these crises.

The globalization of the economy, our increased dependence on trade to maintain our economic prosperity, the growth and proliferation of multinational companies, and the interdependence of the worldwide economic system—all have made the promotion and protection of American economic and commercial interests abroad a predominant function of U.S. diplomacy. Responsibility for these matters falls directly on our ambassadors abroad. How they carry it out in the myriad situations that can arise is amply illustrated in the stories related by the several ambassadors featured in chapter 5.

Lack of Resources

Given the essential role that diplomacy plays in protecting the welfare of the American people, how does one explain the fact—and it is a fact—that for the past decade and a half, the nation has been steadily and drastically reducing the financial and human resources it devotes to this function of our federal government?

"Penny-wise and pound-foolish" is a very apt expression to describe how the U.S. Congress has treated the subject of appropriations to finance U.S. foreign relations in all their aspects. The fault lies as well with successive White House administrations, particularly the role played by the Office of Management and Budget (OMB). While budgetary discipline and ending the deficit were and are most worthy objectives, the handling by politicians of both parties of the so-called 150 Account (shorthand for the 1 percent of the federal budget that funds foreign relations) has been abysmal, considering that America is what everyone seems to agree is "the world's sole remaining superpower," with worldwide responsibilities in security, economics, politics, and other concerns of all humanity. With the president's concurrence, OMB has routinely reduced the request of the secretary of state to fund that department and associated agencies and activities before sending it to Congress, and then Congress has routinely reduced that amount still more.

Neither the White House nor Congress has accepted the principle that diplomacy is our first line of defense. Diplomacy, like defense and intelligence, requires funding as part of the cost of our national security. It should therefore be immune from routine budget cutting. Instead the State Department's appropriation is treated like that of all the domestic departments, agencies, and programs, that is, as "discretionary spending" subject to routine across-the-board percentage cuts and arbitrary budget caps. And when military emergencies occur, as they did in Bosnia in Kosovo, they are funded by emergency appropriations. But nonmilitary international emergencies—unless they are natural disasters—are usually treated as if they did not exist.

The annual foreign relations appropriation (the 150 Account) funds not only the State Department and its Foreign Service but also the public diplomacy and arms control functions (both recently merged into State), foreign aid, our dues and contributions to the United Nations (in arrears for many years) and other international organizations and agencies, the World Bank, the International Monetary Fund, the regional development banks, the Peace Corps, and all other aspects of our relations with the rest of the world.

The state of play this past year between the administration and

Capitol Hill in the annual budget game for fiscal year 2000 is illustrative. With the U.S. gross domestic product at about $9 trillion, the Clinton administration proposed an overall federal budget of $1.8 trillion for the fiscal year that began on October 1, 1999. Of this amount, only a bit more than 1 percent, or $21 billion, was earmarked for spending on international affairs. This represented a reduction of about one-third in real terms from international spending a decade ago. The secretary of state asked for more but was overruled by the OMB.

The Senate and House budget committees then made slashes in the administration's request—the Senate down to $17.7 billion and the House down to $16.4 billion. Secretary Albright correctly labeled these cuts "outrageous and unacceptable." If sustained they would have succeeded in reducing our international funding to half what it was a decade ago. In the end, after arduous negotiations, the president and Congress reached a compromise on a figure of $22.3 billion dollars, still close to 1 percent of the overall federal budget. The president did get Congress to agree to restore some funding for payment of arrears due the United Nations (although spread over three years), peacekeeping, the Wye accords tied to the Middle East peace process, and a small amount for debt relief for poor nations. In the end Congress appropriated about $200 million more than the administration had originally requested, but the figure was lower than the $23.4 billion spending level of the preceding fiscal year, thus continuing the downward trend. Finally acknowledging a lesson from the bombings of our embassies in Kenya and Tanzania, Congress included in the new funding $314 million for improving embassy building security and $254 million for increased operational security (primarily guards and security officers).

As a demonstration of where the administration and Congress place their priorities in the national security area, the November budget negotiations for FY 2000 that finally resolved the major issues with a compromise provided an appropriation of $267.8 billion for the Department of Defense, $4.5 billion more than the administration had originally requested, including several hundred million dollars for an aircraft carrier that the U.S. Navy does not want. As for the intelligence budget, the level of appropriations is classified, but sources on Capitol Hill informed the press that the bill funding the Central Intelligence Agency and 10 other intelligence-gathering agencies and programs received a total of $29.5 billion, a nearly $3 billion increase over the $26.7 billion appropriated the previous year.

In a period of history when the only global power must be fully engaged internationally, and when the international issues the United States must address in its own self-interest increasingly require the building of coalitions among nations and more multilateral negotiation—thus more diplo-macy—America is not providing the appropriations needed to recruit and train skilled, effective diplomats, to maintain and protect our overseas embassies, and to fund America's leadership role in the world.

Our political leaders have failed to properly inform the American peo-ple about the true cost of our involvement with the rest of the world. Over many years public opinion polls have revealed that the average American believes that as much as 20 percent of the federal budget goes for "foreign aid." When asked what the proper figure should be, the same average American says around 5 percent. The fact is that about 1 percent of the federal budget finances not just foreign aid but every aspect of our foreign relations. Knowing that "aid to foreigners" is one of the public's least pop-ular programs, our leaders have shied away from the entire subject. But the foreign affairs budget covers a great deal more than foreign aid and it is high time that the American people learned about the very low cost of carrying out our responsibilities toward the rest of the world.

The Continued Relevance of Diplomacy

Thomas Pickering, the most senior officer in the Foreign Service when he retired in 1997, was almost immediately brought back into service as under secretary of state for political affairs.* His views about the con-tinuing importance of America's diplomatic missions abroad in serving the nation's vital interests were conveyed to the Brookings Institution symposium that helped launch this book.

Today, when America's economic and political health is so closely tied to the rest of the world, it is astonishing that the ques-tion of the relevance of diplomacy can even be raised. It seems obvious to us that the United States needs a more active and well-funded diplomacy to further its expanding interests. Simply put, there are more Americans than ever whose livelihoods depend on trade and investment. There are more American tourists and stu-dents needing assistance and more American businesses that can benefit from our good offices.

From the strategic and political point of view, the United States is engaged in a much more complex world in which effec-tive policies depend upon a deep understanding of foreign cultures

---

* He served as ambassador to Jordan, Nigeria, El Salvador, Israel, the United Nations, India, and the Russian Federation. In Washington he was executive secretary of the State Department and assistant secretary of state for oceans and international environmental and scientific affairs.

and reliable barometers of impending difficulties, be they political or economic. The United States needs more eyes and ears out
there, not fewer.

There is a growing need as well for diplomats serving in new
roles. Perhaps most evident in the Balkans and Eastern Europe,
Foreign Service officers are increasingly serving as peacemakers,
observers, monitors, and managers of assistance programs. They are
literally in the trenches searching for peace and in town halls helping people develop sound democratic and economic practices and
build the institutions of a civil society.

But the question of relevance exists nonetheless, asked by opti-
mists whose enthusiasm for globalization engenders the false
notion that the information age renders diplomats obsolete, as
well as by pessimists who, seeing a confusing world order and
grayer areas of U.S. interest, wonder why we need to bother with
such a messed-up place. In a new way, we are caught between our
historic can-do spirit and vestiges of isolationism. However, the
vast majority of Americans are committed to a strong leadership
role for the United States.

Is diplomacy relevant today? The answer, of course, is yes—
more so than ever. In fact, the issue is really not one of relevance
at all. Questions about the diplomats' role mask other questions.
As a nation we are getting used to a new world and are engaged in
an ongoing discussion of our priorities, resources, and ways of
doing business. In the 20th century the world became ours to rescue and rebuild. Our leadership unquestionably improved the lives
of American citizens, as it shaped a world of expanding security,
freedom, and prosperity.

We must now reconsider what we want the world to look like,
how we want government, business, and private American citizens to shape it, and where we will find partners among other
countries and international institutions. We at the State
Department will do our part by bringing focus to new priorities
and retooling ourselves, even as we maintain our historic
strengths.

If I were a pessimist I might compare the State Department's
to-do list against its budget and consider an immediate second
retirement as my best career choice. But I am an optimist, grateful for the opportunities I have had in foreign affairs and excited
about meeting the challenges before us today, from working for

peace, prosperity, and democracy, to defending our citizens from crime, terrorism, and environmental degradation.

Diplomacy has traditionally been a backstage craft, discreet and anonymous. Unfortunately, that very invisibility means that most Americans do not know how our ambassadors and staffs in the field and in Washington have defended their interests and brought the highest degree of patriotism, professionalism, and sacrifice to the task. In this new period, however, even more than in the past, public diplomacy plays its important part. Anonymity for the practitioners needs to be balanced with a growing need to use the public information tools at our disposal to inform and to solve problems.

Taking that one step further, at the United Nations in New York during and after the Gulf War, we could not have accomplished our mission without public diplomacy. It served to inform and influence the diplomats of other nations directly. It helped keep the American public informed. It was an instant channel to foreign offices and publics around the world and was thus critical in gaining support for our position in the Security Council and in building the coalition that won the war. That was essential diplomacy in a very visible forum.

Diplomacy is not easy today, but Americans, in this era of our prosperity and pre-eminence, can take pride in the world they have helped create. Now we must apply our can-do spirit to the new challenges and opportunities before us. An essential first step is to ensure that America's diplomats have the resources, tools, and training they need to pursue America's interests in the global millennium.

We Need Highly Qualified Ambassadors

The purpose of this book is not to glorify the office of American ambassador, nor to praise individual ambassadors by publicizing their successes. The aim is to demonstrate, by presenting examples from real life, that we still need ambassadors, the best we can obtain. Also, to continue to be effective, the State Department and our embassies require sufficient resources to be able adequately to protect and promote the interests of the United States.

The former ambassadors who participated in the project that produced this book are unanimous in making one final and most important appeal. They call on the president, the secretary of state, and the Foreign Relations Committee of the Senate to work together to ensure that only highly qualified men and women, whether from the career Foreign Service or political appointees, are chosen to represent the United States abroad in ambassadorial assignments. We believe that the stories told here provide evidence that it is essential for our success in dealing with the rest of the world to have only the best people possible heading our diplomatic missions abroad. That means individuals with broad experience, essential skills, and knowledge of the world and of America, above all men and women of sound judgment and probity, with the intellectual and moral courage to propose and promote the policies that will best serve the overall interests of the United States abroad in the new century.

Index

Abu Daud, 65
Adams, Gerry, 51
Aegis naval combat system, 89
Afghanistan, 20-23, 83
Africa, 49, 60, 90
Agency for International Development
  (AID), 26, 28, 79, 105
Agriculture Department, 28
Aideed, Mohammed Farah, 80
Airbus, 106
Air Canada, 55-56
Air Force (U.S.), 78
Albania, 43
Albright, Madeleine, 7, 111
Alcohol, Tobacco, and Firearms Bureau
  (ATF), 33
Algeria, 106
Allende, Salvador, 100-101
Alvarez Machain, Humberto, 58-59
ambassador(s):
  as crisis manager, 65-66, 83-84
  as integrator, 32-33
  as overall coordinator and manager,
    29-30
  as supporter of American business,
    85-86
  diminished influence of, 63
  key role of, 12-13
  leadership of American community by, 15
  limited influence on policy by (but
    uniquely placed), 61-63
  management skills needed for trade
    promotion by, 105-107
  need for highly qualified people to
    serve as, 114-115
  on advantages enjoyed by, 52-53
  on influencing policy at home, 35, and
    abroad, 48-49
  on integrating law enforcement by, 33-34
  on understanding own government, 37,
    41, 51
  roles of summarized, 1-2, 14, 109

statutory duties of, viii, 10-12
American Academy of Diplomacy, 1
American Baptist Society, 18
American community overseas, 12, 15, 17,
  70-73, 77
American Express, 50
American International Assurance (AIA)
  66, 68
Angola, 75
Aquino, Benigno S., Jr., 42
Aquino, Corazon, 70-71
Arafat, Yasir, 80
Armacost, Michael:
  assessing ambassadorial influence on
    policy, 61-63
  on handling trade negotiations, 54
  in Japan, 54
  in Pakistan, 21
  in Philippines, 42, 64
Armed Forces of Liberia (AFL), 73-77
Armitage, Richard, 21, 64
Arms Control and Disarmament Agency
  (ACDA), 46
Asia, 98, 105
Aslam Beg, 23
Association of Southeast Asian Nations
  (ASEAN), 99
Asturias, prince of , 89
Australia, 16, 61, 67

Baker, James, 3, 76, 78
Baldrige, Malcolm, 92-93
Balkans, 113
Basques, 89
Bechtel Corporation, 106
Bhutto, Benazir, 22-23
Bishop, James:
  dealing with political and military
    violence and chaos, 73-78
  in Liberia, 73-77
  in Somalia, 77-78
Black Hawk helicopter, 88-89

"Black September," 65
Blanchard, James:
    in Canada, 29-30, 54-58
    as coordinator and manager, 29-30
    on negotiating a bilateral aviation
        agreement, 54-58
Boeing, 106
Bohlen, Avis, 46
Bolivia, 24-28
Bonner, Elena, 4
Border Patrol, 25
Bosnia, 30, 87, 110
Bosworth, Stephen, 42
Boutros-Ghali, Boutros, 81
Bowie, Robert R.:
    key role of ambassadors, 12-13
Brazil, 16, 27, 38
Brooke, Edward, 40
Brookings Institution, 1, 42, 112
Bruce, David, 40
Bureau of Inter-American Affairs (State
    Department), 101
Bush, George, 3-5, 11, 23, 49, 76, 78-79

Camarena, Enrique, 58
Canada, 29-30, 43, 54-58, 67
Cardenas, Lazaro, 99
Carlucci, Frank:
    on changing policy toward Portugal,
        38-42, 62
    at NSC, 20
    in Portugal, 38-42
Central Intelligence Agency (CIA), 21, 25,
    46, 51-53, 68, 75, 111
Chamber of Commerce (U.S.), 103
Charter 77 (Czechoslovakia), 43
Chiapas, 94
Chile, 64, 100-101
China, 16
Chirac, Jacques, 89
Citgo, 102
Clark Air Force Base, 70
Clark, Ramsey, 74
"clientitis," 34
Clinton, Bill, 58, 79, 81, 87
Clinton letter, 10
CNN, 6-7, 18, 63
Coast Guard (U.S.), 25
Cold War, 1-3, 8, 10, 86-87, 93, 105-107

Commerce Department, 28, 46, 87, 92
Common Agricultural Policy (EU), 90
communications, changes in, 5-6
Communists, 38-39, 70, 86
Communist Youth League (Italy), 86
Conference on Security and Cooperation in
    Europe (CSCE), 42-48
Congress (U.S.), 9-10, 13-16, 21, 23, 29,
    35, 37, 40, 42, 44-48, 50, 52, 62-64,
    103, 110-112, 114
Constable, Elinor:
    assisting American companies, 90-93
    improving the business climate, 90-93
    in Kenya, 18-20, 90-93
    rescuing a judge, 18-20
consular affairs, 15-18
consular posts, 16-17
corruption, 85, 90-93
country team, 11, 26, 33-34
Creole (Petroleum), 100
Crist, George, 21
crony capitalism, 90, 94
Crowe, William, 9, 64
CSCE Commission of Congress, 47-48
Cuba, 55, 75
Customs Service, 33

DeConcini, Dennis, 48
Defense Department, 21-22, 46, 52, 64, 111
Defense Security Assistance Agency (DSAA), 97
Delta Airlines, 56, 72
Democratic Party, 5
"Desert Shield," 77
Dillon, Robert:
    in Malaysia, 66-70
    on managing a hostage crisis, 66-70
diplomacy:
    19th century, 5
    continued relevance of, 112-114
    economic and commercial, 86-87
    multilateral, 42-48
    resources for, 8-10, 14, 110-112
    shuttle, 7
    special envoys, 7, 13
Dobrynin, Anatoly, 3
Doe, Samuel K., 73-77
Dominican Republic, 18
Drug Enforcement Administration (DEA),
    24, 26, 33, 58-59

Dubar, Henry, 73-74
Dulles, John Foster, 7

Eagleburger, Lawrence, 3, 38, 41
East Asia, 60, 64, 85
Eastern Europe, 43-44, 52, 98, 113
Egypt, 32-33, 65, 71-73
Eid, Guy, 65
Eisenhower, Dwight, 7
Eizenstat, Stuart, 87
El Salvador, 83
embassy staff, 12-14, 20-25, 30-31
Euro, 89
Eurocopter, 88
Europe, 30, 39, 43, 60, 85, 87
European Bureau (State Department),
    44-47, 49
European Union (EU), 41, 87-90
Exxon, 99

Federal Aviation Administration (FAA), 33
Federal Bureau of Investigation (FBI), 33
first line of defense, 9, 110
Forbes Park, 71
Ford, Gerald, 39
Foreign Assistance Act, 100
Foreign Commercial Service, 87
Foreign Service of the United States, 24, 29,
    34-35, 77, 110, 112-113, 115
France, 16, 45, 72, 86, 88-89
Frankel, Marvin, 19

Gallucci, Robert, 7
Galvin, Jack, 27
Gardner, Richard:
    in Italy, 86
    on managing economic and commercial
        diplomacy, 86-90
    in Spain, 86-90
General Agreement on Tariffs and Trade
    (GATT), 50, 87
General Dynamics, 97
General Motors, 106
Georgetown University, 89
Germany, 16, 45, 52, 56, 72, 86, 88-89
Ghulum Ishaq Khan (GIK), 21, 23
Goldberg, Arthur, 44
Gonçalves, Vasco, 38
Gonzales Amendment, 100

Gonzalez, Felipe, 87, 89
Gorbachev, Mikhail, 3-4, 43-45
Grenada, 89
Gulf War, 32, 52, 71-73, 77, 80, 114

Habib, Philip, 53
Haig, Alexander, 40
Haiti, 18, 30
Hakimulla Khan, 21
Harrop, William:
    on first line of defense, 9
    on resources, 8-10
    on security, 9
Havel, Vaclav, 41
Helsinki Final Act, 43
Hickenlooper Amendment, 100
Hirsch, John, 79
Holbrooke, Richard, 7
Hollywood, 88
Howe, Jonathan, 81
Hoyer, Steny, 48
Hughes Corporation, 98
human rights, 42-48, 76, 94
Hummel, Arthur:
    a contrarian view on policy influence, 63
Hussein, Saddam, 71-72, 78

Immigration and Naturalization Service
    (INS), 33
India, 13, 16, 20-22, 98
Indonesia, 98, 105
Internally Displaced Persons (IDPs), 76
International Affairs Strategic Plan (U.S.),
    103-104
International Committee of the Red Cross
    (ICRC), 76
International Monetary Fund (IMF), 110
International Petroleum Company, 99
Iran, 20, 83
Iraq, 78, 80
Israel, 13, 65
Italy, 16, 86-88

Jackson, Richard, 67
Japan, 16-17, 54, 67-69, 81-82, 85-86, 96,
    105
Japanese Red Army (JRA), 67-69
Johnson, Rudolph, 74-75
Johnston, Robert, 79, 81

Johnstone, Craig:
  on domestic public diplomacy, 13-14
  on management skills needed by
    ambassadors, 105-107
  on resources for diplomacy, 14
  on supporting America's prosperity,
    103-105
Jones, James R.:
  on expanding the commercial
    relationship, 93-96
  in Mexico, 93-96
Jordan, 65
Justice Department, 51

Kampelman, Max, 44
Kennan, George, 53
Kennedy letter, 10
Kenya, 9, 18-20, 90-93, 111
Kenyatta, Jomo, 91
Kissinger, Henry, 7, 39, 43, 48, 64, 68
Kitty Hawk aircraft carrier, 96-97
Kobe, 81-82
Korey, William, 44
Kosovo, 8-9, 110
Ku Klux Klan, 19
Kuwait, 83
Kyoto, 16, 68

Lake Maracaibo, 100, 102
LaPorta, Al, 68
Latin America, 33, 41, 60, 64, 99, 101
Lawyers Committee for Human Rights, 19
Lebanon, 53, 66, 69, 80, 83
Lesotho, 18
Liberia, 73-77, 83
Libya, 68
Lockheed Martin, 89, 97
Low, Stephen:
  examples of changing a president's
    mind, 63-64

Macomber, William, 65
Madhi, Mohamed Ali, 80
Mahoney, Haynes, 68
Makati, 70-71
Malacanang Palace, 70
Malaysia, 66-70, 96-99
Malta, 44
management by objectives, 25-29

Marcos, Ferdinand, 42, 64
Marines (U.S.), 66, 70, 77-78, 80, 82
Matlock, Jack, 53
McDonald's, 83
McDonnell Douglas, 97-98
McPherson, Peter, 74
Mexico, 33-34, 55, 58-60, 93-96, 99
Middle East, 7, 13, 20, 32, 71, 73, 78, 87,
  100, 111
missionaries, 18-19
mission statement, 12
Mitchell, George, 7
Moi, Daniel arap, 19, 90-93
Mondale, Walter:
  consular posts in Japan, 16-17
  crisis management in Japan, 81-82
  in Japan, 16-17, 81-82
Moore, George Curtis, 65
Morocco, 106
Motion Picture Association, 88
Motley, Tony:
  on American community overseas, 12
  on country team, 11
  on duties and roles of ambassadors, 10-12
  on embassy staff, 12
  on mission statement, 12
  on presidential letters, 11
Mount Pinatubo, 70
Munich Olympic Games, 65
Murata, Kyohei, 69
Murray, Vera, 5
Mutual and Balanced Force Reductions
  (MBFR), 46

Nagoya, 16
national security:
  and diplomacy, 9, 64
  budget for, 10, 110-112
National Security Council (NSC), 13, 20,
  28, 46-47, 52, 64
NATO, 6, 8-9, 39-40, 44, 86-88
Navy (U.S.), 25, 63, 97, 111
Navy Seals, 70, 78
Negroponte, John:
  on "clientitis," 34
  on handling a crisis in the bilateral
    relationship, 58-60
  on integrating law enforcement and on
    unilateralism, 33-34

in Mexico, 33-34, 58-60
New Transatlantic Agenda, 87
New Zealand, 16, 67
Nicaragua, 31
Nixon, Richard, 64-65, 100
"No Distribution" (NODIS), 52-53
Noel, Cleo A., Jr., 65
non-governmental organizations (NGOs), 47
North American Free Trade Agreement (NAFTA), 29-30, 55, 58, 95
Northern Ireland, 7, 51
North Korea, 7
Northwest Airlines, 56

Oakley, Phyllis, 20
Oakley, Robert:
  on diplomatic input to an international humanitarian intervention, 78-81
  on leading an embassy that lost its leader, 20-24
  in Pakistan, 20-24
  in Somalia, 78-81
Office of Management and Budget (OMB), 40, 110-111
Okinawa, 82
Oman, 78
O'Neill, Tip, 83
Onn, Hussein, 67
"open skies," 55, 57
"Operation Desert Storm," 80
"Operation Provide Comfort," 80
"Operation Restore Hope," 79
Organization of American States (OAS), 64
Organization of Petroleum Exporting Countries (OPEC), 102
Orinoco Tar Belt, 101-102
Osaka, 81-82
Ottawa Airport, 57

Pacific Roundtable, 99
Pakistan, 20-24, 83
Pakistan People's Party, 22-23
Palestine Liberation Organization (PLO), 80
Panama, 26
Panama Canal, 63-64
Peace Corps, 70, 110
Perez, Carlos Andres, 100, 103

Perkins, Edward:
  in Australia, 61
  on management by objectives, 28-29
  on using public diplomacy, 61
Persian Gulf, 77, 87, 97
Peru, 31-32, 99
Peterson, Katherine, 18
Petroleos de Venezuela-Petroven, 101-102
Philippines, 42, 64, 70-71
Pickering, Thomas:
  on the continued relevance of diplomacy, 112-114
Platt, Nicholas:
  on dealing with internal chaos, 70-71
  in Philippines, 70-71
policy dissent, 30-31
Popov, Gavril, 4
Portugal, 38-42
Powell, Colin, 20, 23, 52, 79
Pressler Amendment, 21, 23
Price, Charles, 49
public diplomacy:
  abroad, 50
  in Australia, 61
  in Canada, 57
  domestic, 13-14
  at the United Nations, 114

Quainton, Anthony:
  on conflict over security rules, 31-32
  on leadership, 30-32
  in Nicaragua, 31
  in Peru, 31-32
  on policy dissent, 30-31
Quayle, Dan, 59
Quebec referendum, 29

Raphel, Arnold, 20-21
Reagan, Ronald, 23, 42, 64, 75
resources:
  for foreign affairs, 8-10, 14, 110-112
  of non-State agencies, 63
  150 Account, 110-112
Ridgway, Rozanne, 46
Robertsfield Airport, 75
Robinson, Randall, 64
Rosenthal, Andres, 59-60
Ross, Dennis, 7
Rotary Club, 60

Rowell, Edward:
  in Bolivia, 24-28
  on management by objectives, 25-28
Rumsfeld, Donald, 39
Russia, 16, 32, 96-98
Ryan, Mary:
  on missionaries, 18
  on protection of American citizens
    abroad, 17
  in Swaziland, 60-61
  on warden networks, 17-18
  on women's issues, 60-61

Sakharov, Andrei, 43-44
Salinas, Carlos, 59
Santer, Jacques, 87
Sapporo, 16
Saudi Arabia, 65
Scott, Stuart, 38
Scowcroft, Brent, 23
security:
  of diplomatic premises, 9, 111
  vs. openness, 31-32
Seitz, Raymond G. H.:
  on briefing editors, 50-51
  on influencing British policy, 49-53
  as a "punching bag," 51
  in the United Kingdom, 49-53
Shafei, Ghazali, 67-69
Shevardnadze, Eduard A., 45
Shlaudeman, Harry W.:
  on handling expropriation of American
    property, 99-103
  in Venezuela, 99-103
Shultz, George, 20-21, 45-47, 51, 74, 90
Siad Barre, 77
Sigur, Gaston, 64

Sikorsky Aircraft Corporation (United
  Technologies), 88-89
Sinn Fein (Northern Ireland), 51
Soares, Mario, 38-41
Social Democrats (Portugal), 41
Socialist Party (Portugal), 38-41
Solana, Javier, 87
Solidarity (Poland), 43
Somalia, 77-81, 83
South Africa, 31, 64, 90

South America, 58
South Asia, 36
SouthCom (U.S. Southern Command), 27
Southeast Asia, 98-99
Soviet Union, 3-5, 20, 23, 43-45, 47-48,
  52-53, 75, 78, 86
Spain, 86-90
Spain, king of, 89
Sri Lanka, 68
Standard Oil of New Jersey, 100
Stebbins, Robert, 67, 69
Strauss, Robert:
  in the Soviet Union, 3-5, 61
Streator, Edward, 40
Sudan, 65-66
Suez Canal, 32
Sullivan, Joseph G., 83
Supreme Court (U.S.), 59
Swaziland, 60-61
Sweden, 66-67, 69
Swing, William, 18

Tanzania, 9, 111
Taylor, Charles, 75
Thailand, 98, 105
Third World, 60
Tokyo subway system, 82
Trade Representative (U.S.), 28
transportation, changes in, 7
Transportation Department, 56
Treasury Department, 28, 40
Triton Energy, 98
Turkey, 69

Uganda, 83
Underhill, Frank, 66
Unified International Task Force (UNITAF),
  79, 81
United Kingdom, 5-6, 16, 45, 49-53, 56,
  67, 86, 88
United Nations (UN), 9, 28, 81, 110-111,
  114
United States Information Agency (USIA),
  27, 106
UNRWA (UN relief agency for Palestinian
  refugees), 69
UN Security Council, 78-79, 114
USAir, 56

Valenti, Jack, 88
Vance, Cyrus, 7
Velvet Revolution (Czechoslovakia), 44
Venezuela, 99-103
Vienna, 42-48
Vietnam, 6, 9, 27, 31, 80
Vision 2020 (Malaysia), 98
Voice of America, 75

warden networks, 17-18
Warsaw Pact, 44
Whitehead, John, 28
Wilhelm, Charles, 80
Wise, Sam, 48
Wisner, Frank:
   in Egypt, 32-33, 71-73
   in India, 36-37
   on influencing policy in Washington,
     36-37
   on integrating disparate goals, 32-33
   on maintaining American presence
     during war, 71-73
   on special case of Israel, 13

Wolf, John S.:
   on doing business in Asia, 98-99
   in Malaysia, 96-99
   on promoting business opportunities,
     96-98
Wolfowitz, Paul, 64
women's issues, 60-61
World Bank, 110
World Trade Organization (WTO), 87, 104
Wye accords, 111

Yeltsin, Boris, 4
Yokohama Advanced Japanese Language
   School, 16
Yugoslavia, 7

Zia al Haq, 20-22
Zimmermann, Warren:
   at Vienna CSCE review conference, 42-48
Zinni, Anthony, 80